RAISING A
SUPERSTAR

RAISING A SUPERSTAR

Simple Strategies to Bring Out the
BRILLIANCE in Every Child

TERRI A. KHONSARI

Copyright © 2007 by Terri Khonsari

All rights reserved. No part of this book may be used or reproduced in any manner whatsoever without prior written consent of the author, except as provided by the United States of America copyright law.

Published by Advantage, Charleston, South Carolina.
Member of Advantage Media Group.

ADVANTAGE is a registered trademark and the Advantage colophon is a trademark of Advantage Media Group, Inc.

Printed in the United States of America

ISBN: 978-1-59932-046-5
Library of Congress Control Number: 2007932271

> Most Advantage Media Group titles are available at special quantity discounts for bulk purchases for sales promotions, premiums, fundraising, and educational use. Special versions or book excerpts can also be created to fit specific needs.
>
> For more information, please write: Special Markets, Advantage Media Group, P.O. Box 272, Charleston, SC 29402 or call 1.866.775.1696.

DEDICATION

To all parents who are doing their best to help
their children become the best they can be.

&

To Niloufar, my beloved daughter:
My pride in you is only exceeded by my love for you.

TABLE OF CONTENTS

9 | ACKNOWLEDGEMENTS

11 | INTRODUCTION:
From Iran to America

19 | CHAPTER 1:
What Makes a Superstar Child?

43 | CHAPTER 2:
School and the Superstar

59 | CHAPTER 3:
Superstar Habits for Life

79 | CHAPTER 4:
The Superstar Abroad

91 | CHAPTER 5:
The Selfless Superstar

109 | CHAPTER 6:
The Superstar Family

125 | CHAPTER 7:
The Well-Rounded Superstar

ACKNOWLEDGMENTS

There are so many incredible people in my life that I could take 100 pages to thank them all. Here I will just take a few...

- To my parents—Thank you for all the love you gave me. Thank you for raising me with a passion to contribute. Thank you for everything you did to help me become who I am today.

- To my daughter, Nilou—Thank you for giving me energy, love and pride every minute of my life just by being who you are; and thank you for your support in editing and creating this book.

- To my wonderful husband, Hamid—Thank you for your support and patience while I was writing and working on the book days, nights and weekends.

- To my fantastic friends and family—Thank you for cheering me on and thank you for all your encouragement and words of support. Thank you for your faith and the excitement that you have shown during almost two years of work on this book.

- To Mark Victor Hansen—Thank you for hosting the mega events that inspired me to finally write this book.

- To my writing coach, Ann McIndoo—Thank you for helping me get the ideas out of my head and onto paper.

- To Tim Vandehey, my incredible editor—Thank you for helping me make the book flow and become a book that can change people's lives.

- To Adam Witty and Advantage Media Group, my publisher —Thank you for all your hard work and personal care and attention in getting this book published.

- To my readers—Thank you for trusting me in this journey of growth and in the process of unleashing your children's potential.

INTRODUCTION:
From Iran to America

Let's define the superstar first. What is a superstar? For the purpose of this book a superstar is a well-rounded individual who shines in different areas of life and chooses to be their best at everything they attempt. Superstars are happy, healthy, and fulfilled individuals. They sample many different areas of life and enjoy the act of discovery. Superstars' interests are broad. They live life as an exciting whole. They engage in their career, sports, arts, music and many other pursuits. They care for the community and the world as they care for themselves. Superstars are driven self-starters; they are able to create a balance between the many different things that they do to keep mentally and emotionally fit. Being perfect in one thing doesn't make you a superstar, at least for the purposes of this book.

Most importantly, a superstar takes hold of life and lives every area with passion and joy. For the superstar, the journey and the tests that come with it are as much the point as the destination. I have written this book to share with you my insights on raising your children to be superstars, based largely on my own experiences with my extraordinary daughter, Nilou. I know that as her mother, I am hardly objective, but I think you will see as we journey together that she is an example of the fundamental premise of superstar children: they are made, not born. Every child has the potential to be a superstar, because superstardom means being the best you can be and maximizing your potential in every area of your life—not just the ones where you have natural gifts. That is what my daughter has done with my help, and I hope to share some of our wisdom with you and your children.

Why Nilou is a Superstar

As I write this book, my daughter is 23 and studying at Georgetown Law School with the goal of practicing international law in the area of human rights. Since she was very young, she knew that she wanted to contribute to the world and make a difference in the global community. She is an academic star.

She has also made herself into a model of physical fitness. She runs marathons and ultra marathons in the U.S. and all over the world; she also races in triathlons. Her next athletic goal is to do the Ironman Triathlon in New Zealand. She is serious about sports, physical and mental health. She mostly eats organic and healthy food, respects her body, and takes care of her health.

Nilou has helped non-profits and non-governmental organizations as a volunteer, and has contributed to our Bay Area community in many ways, such as conducting research, teaching, and producing legal briefs. She is the President of the Human Rights group and Vice President of Amnesty International at Georgetown Law School. If there is a need - from hunger to health and education - she is determined to help out. She spoke five languages (English, Farsi, French, German and Spanish) fluently by the time she was 18 and graduated from South Side High School in New York. In the U.S., where few natural-born citizens rarely speak a second language, this is exceptional.

She has traveled to six continents and more than 30 countries, most of them with me as a child and as a teenager. As a result, she is highly aware of other cultures and people, and interested in the world as a community. Most of her trips took place before she even went to college, and she continued her international journey after she entered university. Most gratifying to me, Nilou loves the human family and remains "dangerously positive" toward life. She is adaptive and confident. She creates excitement and joy in whatever she does and attracts other people to her energy. She feels incredible love for everyone on earth. That love is what drives her to excel in so many areas, knowing that the more she is capable of, the more likely she is to help others.

Again, I am hardly an objective observer. I love and admire my daughter and think she is the greatest person I know. But she didn't just spring from the womb as a superstar. I pushed her and encouraged her, and she pushed herself. No superstar child is an accident. Nilou's journey began with my own journey from Iran to America and the many obstacles that shaped us both.

A Woman without a Country

I was almost twenty-two when my then-husband left me and our daughter at a train station in Munich, Germany. Born and raised in Iran, I married when I was nineteen and had Nilou a year-and-a-half later. Fifteen months later, my husband and I moved from Iran to Germany and after another three months my husband broke the news—he wanted a divorce. Decision time! What would I do?

I decided to stay in Germany and be a divorced single mom instead of running back to my home in Iran. Unfortunately, I could not speak German; all I had was a high school diploma from Tehran and a toddler who didn't know what was going on. I had no idea what to do first or next. I knew I had big dreams: I wanted to learn German, go to university and continue my education, grow and become a better person who could do bigger things for society and myself. Most of all, I wanted my daughter to be a superstar. I wanted to raise an extraordinary individual who would help change the world for the better.

So, instead of focusing on how irresponsible her father was, I did what women have done since time began: I focused on making the best of things. I went to school and learned German, I went to university, and I enrolled Nilou in a million different activities after school and on weekends: ballet, piano, tennis, Farsi, painting, you name it. I worked, studied and entertained my growing little girl at the same time, and I had fun.

As time passed, she began to develop her own interests separate from what I was trying to get her involved in. Things like changing from ballet and tennis to jazz dance and basketball. We had a standing rule in our home: laziness and doing nothing and watching TV, instead of being active physically and mentally, were not allowed. Nilou could choose what she wanted to do, but she had to try it for awhile before she was allowed to quit. So she was always active in one thing or another, but she was never forced to do anything that did not captivate her. Often her interests were not my interests, but that was not the point; I always made sure not to confuse my goals with hers. Parents should not live vicariously through their children.

Off to North America

So life went on. We had lots of fun living in Europe and traveling to different countries and cities for long weekends or longer vacations. Nilou started to learn about the differences in European countries and developed an interest in other cultures and languages at an early age.

We then moved to Canada for a few cold winter months and from there to the U.S. in the Spring of 1996. Now we were immigrants to three different countries; Nilou had gone to ten different schools by the time she completed high school. So-called experts will tell you that so much change in the educational environment is not good for a child, but she thrived on it. She was stimulated by the new people she was meeting and the new things she was learning. To me, how a child handles such change depends on how you, the parent, make it sound—how you paint the picture of relocating for your child. You have the power to shape your child's perspective on life's events. You can make the worst thing be the best thing in their lives, or turn normal happenings into tragedy and trauma, depending on what perspective you pass onto your children.

My approach was to say, "Wow! You get a chance to make even more great friends and keep your old friends too!" It was all a process of enrichment and growth for both of us. I had my master's degree; but, again, I had language problems and no work experience in the U.S.; and I faced all the legal obstacles new immigrants face.

Eventually, I started working for United Airlines in management, and I took advantage of my flight benefits to take Nilou to places like China, Egypt and Australia so she could learn about the differences in history, culture, people and ways of living.

More than a decade later, here I sit, married again to a wonderful physician and living in the beautiful San Francisco Bay Area, writing about my experience raising my daughter -- and how everyone can raise a superstar. Every now and then I stop and look back at the experiences we shared -- the uncertainty and the adventure and the discovery. I know that my superstar daughter would not be who she has become today without those experiences, both the challenging and the rewarding ones. Neither would I be who I am. And I am grateful.

What is Within Your Children?

This book is a guide for all parents: those who are starting out, who are frustrated with the teenage attitude, or who worry about what will happen when their children go into the world. In these pages, I will share with you some of the lessons, rules and methods that I used with my daughter that helped her develop discipline and confidence, work hard, give to others and look for joy in all things.

There is a light at the end of the tunnel of the most maddening parenting experience, and I am going to show it to you. There are many simple things you can do to bring out the superstar in your child. My goal is to help as many parents as possible raise superstars who fan out to different careers and interests, and to show you that some simple steps, applied with persistence and love, can make all the difference.

I hope my story is a small help in the process, and that my book will make a worthwhile contribution to your parenting and raising great children. Enjoy it and love your children, communicate with them, give them confidence and inspire them to live with passion.

This book is for you, and I would love to know what you think and to hear your own stories. Please send any questions or stories to me at terri@RaisingASuperstar.com.

Thank you for joining me on this journey.

CHAPTER ONE:
What Makes a Superstar Child?

You are the bows from which your children as living arrows are sent forth.

— *Kahlil Gibran*

Superstar children are made, not born. Each child is born with innate talents and differences, things that they can do better than most of their peers and things that they cannot do as easily as other children. Capitalizing only on natural gifts does not make a child a superstar. Superstardom is less about *ability* and more about *attitude*. This is why I have said that any child can learn to become a superstar, because attitudes are learned. By imparting superstar attitudes and ways of thinking to your children from the time they learn to communicate, you help them develop habits that lead to success in everything they try.

Success doesn't mean they will be the best at what they do; they may not be. Success means they do their best and give their best in everything they do. They may fail at something or discover they are no better at it than everyone else. Success is not measured in trophies. It is measured by how hard your children work, how much passion and determination they bring to everything they attempt, and how enthusiastic they are in seeking their endeavors without fear.

> *Champions aren't made in gyms. Champions are made from something they have deep inside them - a desire, a dream, a vision. They have to have last-minute stamina, they have to be a little faster, they have to have the skill and the will. But the will must be stronger than the skill.*
> — *Muhammad Ali*

Superstar children live that sentiment every day. They come to the world with big ideas and big expectations and they know that sampling everything at the table is much more important than eating only one dish they know they will love. Starting early, teach your children to have a ravenous appetite for life and discovery by making the following principles part of daily life.

Parents should not let their children be OK with average or below-average achievement... if you can see that they did not give their absolute best. I am not suggesting being a harsh taskmaster and punishing them for failure; not at all. But encourage them to always give their best and dream big in whatever they try to do. Oprah Winfrey once said, "Doing your best at this moment puts you in the best place the next moment." That's right. Encourage and push your children to do their best. However, do not force your kids to do things that they don't like. Encourage them to try new things, and when they gravitate toward something naturally, help them set high standards for themselves. Failure is no shame; lack of effort is.

Look at the Visionaries

Look at big thinkers throughout history, people like Eleanor Roosevelt, Bill Gates and Thomas Edison, and read about their lives. What was their vision and mission? Did they walk easy paths to their success, or did they face obstacles and people who told them they could not succeed? No matter what happened, people like these did not set out to build something small. They set out to change the world. That's what your children should be doing. Always remind them if they aim for stars and miss, they'll still reach the moon. Most people don't even reach for the ceiling! How can they ever expect even to get to the roof? Use metaphors and stories when you talk with your children and help them understand that their big dreams are nothing to hide, but to grow.

In our adventures together, Nilou and I always went after more. We never settled. Every time we moved, we planned for bigger and more and we achieved it. We were criticized by family members and friends, who asked us why we didn't just stop and live like everyone else. "Just be normal," they said. My answer was always the same: why would we want to limit ourselves when we can be so much more? My daughter learned that lesson at a young age: never settle for less. Find one thing, become great at it, then find something else and grow more. Make life extraordinary.

It's Not about Money

Oh, please do not make money the end goal! Your kids will be very unhappy. Those who live only to make money, never achieve true success. True success comes with discovering your purpose, living with meaning and passion, and making a difference in the lives of others. If you look at many people who became super-rich, they had a vision that was much bigger than money. They had a mission for their life. They started with an idea that would make a difference.

Think about Bill Gates. His vision was having every person in America own a computer. He never said, "I want to be the world's richest man." That would have never gotten him where he is now. He had a big vision and he followed it for years. Think about others who have transformed the world: artists, inventors, scientists, political leaders, and entrepreneurs. None of them started by saying, "I want to make the most money." Teach your children to have big dreams and the money will follow.

Leadership

Being a leader is something that can be learned but rarely is. Some people learn it later, while others never learn. Leadership is not giving orders and wielding authority. It is inspiring others to pursue a common goal and be their best. Most of us learn simply to follow as early as when we are in elementary school, because we all have the strong need to fit in and be part of the group. But children can learn to be leaders.

To teach your children leadership you must first become a leader yourself. How can you expect them to walk to the front of the line if all you are doing is copying the rest of the crowd, not taking any essential leadership steps in your life? Children watch what you do and they learn from what you are doing. If you are creating better circumstances and greater fulfillment in your family life by taking the bold steps of a leader, your youngsters will notice. First, become what you say, then expect them to do it. Nilou always saw our life as an example of my leading and never considered us being followers.

When she was fifteen, Nilou went to the Young Women's Leadership Camp. The camp was designed to help girls become leaders in society, and it was not easy to get accepted. We received an invitation six months before, saying those who were interested needed to send an application. These girls had to answer many questions and write long essays about challenging topics and about their lives. Selection took months. The camp finally selected thirty girls out of about 1,000 applicants; Nilou was one of them.

They say surround yourself with people who you want to be like; learn from them and you will become one of them eventually. These thirty elite girls were taught for one full week, day and night, how to take charge of their lives, lead, set tremendous goals, and make plans how to achieve those goals.

They also learned a great deal about the history of women in leadership. This really impacted Nilou. She learned how to organize, how to initiate new things, how to think independently, and how to go for the best and the biggest. She learned about women who made a difference in history, science, and politics. She came back powerful and energetic, with lots of passion and great ideas. We enjoyed endless hours of conversations about things that she learned and things that she was planning to do.

The Right Direction

Most parents like to send their kids to camp to keep them busy and to make sure they have fun in the summer, which is wonderful. I did the same. Once I sent my daughter to an adventure camp where she got a taste of rock-climbing, white water rafting, canoeing and hiking. But keeping busy was never the goal; that was never a problem. Learning and becoming a better person while having fun was the main goal for us.

If you want to have a superstar, then you have to take appropriate action and plant the leadership seeds when they are young. If you let your kids do what everybody else does because of peer pressure or social mores, and then expect them to become something different from everyone else, you will be disappointed. We take on the look of the waters in which we swim. Developing leadership means sending your children off in new directions, doing things other kids aren't, giving them the means to grow in new ways.

One of the things Nilou did after this camp, when she came back brimming with ideas and goals and energy, was starting a rock-climbing club at her school. She said, "I love rock climbing, and there is no rock-climbing club in my school." She was active in so many clubs—Debate, Astronomy, Red Cross, Youth Decide, Youth Court, French, Spanish, you name it. At that time I had to work all the time and could not drive her to the rock-climbing gym. The only way she would be able to go was by starting the club and getting the school bus to take the group after school or on weekends. So she did it. She saw a need and took responsibility for starting something to meet it. That's leadership.

One day she told me she loved-rock climbing for more than the physical challenge and the adrenaline rush. She sees it as being like life. As we near our goals the climb gets harder and harder and we run low on energy, especially when we are near the top. But by looking down and seeing how far we have gotten, then looking up at how little there is left before the finish, we regain our energy. Every step we take gets us one step closer to the top, and the feeling when we get there is better than anything else we can experience.

Persistence

I have not seen a single successful person who never failed. I have never seen a truly successful person who gave up easily. If you have never failed in your life, you haven't been risking enough. True giants embrace the idea of failure; they know the lessons they learn will eventually fuel their success.

One day, one of my colleagues at United Airlines told me she had never failed. More to the point, she had never tried anything at which she could possibly fail. She was so proud of herself. I was horrified. She still has the same job after ten years, while everyone else moved up. She was comfortable and felt secure in her position, and she would never rise higher. With stardom and success come risk taking, courage, and knowing you have some battles to fight.

Teach your children not to give up, to keep moving forward rather than maintaining the status quo. Train them not to play it safe (I don't refer to actual physical safety, of course), but to stick their necks out. As the old saying goes, "Go out on a limb, that's where the fruit is." We all failed at first, when we were children learning to walk. We tried and we fell. If we'd given up, where would we be? A world of crawling adults, a ridiculous picture!

A Rebel with a Cause

A couple of years after we moved to America, I wanted a real job. I decided I would get a small job with a large company and move up from there. I started with a small job at United Airlines and planned to move up as quickly as possible. I was still on probation, two months into the company, and I started sending applications for higher positions.

CHAPTER 1 - WHAT MAKES A SUPERSTAR CHILD?

I had just finished my training for the job I was supposed to do when I started to look at better and bigger job openings. I started sending applications to every management job that I felt I could do and that would excite me. I went to interview after interview and I failed them all. People were making fun of me. In my colleagues' eyes I was a person who thought she could be in management just because she had a degree from Germany. I didn't know my place. They were saying things like, "Who does she think she is?" "She has no experience." "She just got this job." "She has no airline experience and she wants to run the company?" "She wants to be in a management position and be in charge of hundreds of people? Who does she think she is?"

I didn't listen, though it was hard. I knew I could make it but I didn't know how much longer it would take! It was difficult: going on so many interviews, flying from city to city, going to the interview all dressed up, ready and prepared, thinking I had all the right answers, knowing I'd done well, then finding out two days later I hadn't gotten the position. My inexperience continued to work against me.

Nilou was right there with me. At fourteen, it was her first time experiencing the rejection that I had experienced many times. It may have been harder on her than on me. She watched what I was going through, the way I felt, the nights that I cried and asked myself, "When?" And I knew as I struggled that I would never quit, not only because I knew I could do the job but also I would never give up because I didn't want my little girl to think it was OK to quit. This was a key life lesson for Nilou. I had to persist and reach my goal. That kept me going.

I didn't know how many resumes I had sent out within United until my manager one day called me. In three months, I had sent out 250 resumes for 250 different jobs. I was stunned. She told me she had received a call from the Human Resources, who had said they wanted to know who this person was who had sent so many resumes and had gone to so many interviews. So for my next interview, a week later, an HR person was sent along to check me out. The interview went well. They usually did. I had a vision of what I could do in this company, whether anyone liked it or not.

A couple days of later the call came: once again I didn't get the job. I called the HR person and asked for her feedback. She said she thought I was amazing! She found the way I looked at work -- at the company and the industry -- very interesting, and she told me that I would get something soon. My current position, she said, was not the right place for me. That was like a boost of new energy for my tired ego and emotions.

At my very next interview, I got the job—an even better position than the one I had been seeking previously! All the people who made fun of me came and said congratulations. I celebrated the victory with my daughter and we talked for hours about the importance of persistence and not giving up.

Ten Thousand Ways That Won't Work

A person who never made a mistake never tried anything new.

—Albert Einstein

I had been on eleven interviews in eleven different cities and states before the twelfth that got me the job. Before I reached my goal, it was painful. Once I found my new position, I saw that my prior failures had led me to this new place. I stopped referring to things as failures; they became steps for getting closer to my goal. The lesson was unmistakable: if I had stayed where I was "supposed" to, I would have not been where I am today. I would have given others the power to decide my future.

How many times have you shown your children that you would not give up? Remember those times, make a list of them, and discuss them in your next family meeting or on the next long drive you take with your daughter or son. They will remember your lesson, because you have lived it. Remind them that failure is not about coming up short in an endeavor, but in letting that temporary setback discourage you from trying again. Remind them of what Thomas Edison said when a friend asked him if he was discouraged after failing in nearly 10,000 different attempts to invent the electricity: "I didn't fail ten thousand times. I successfully eliminated, ten thousand times, materials and combinations which would not work. I am ten thousand steps closer to the goal."

Exercise

Write down some of the instances in which you experienced failure but didn't give up and resumed moving toward your goals.

Your failure

How you recovered

The result

Encourage Role Models

Role models are essential, because children learn much of their behavior by emulating others. So your child's future superstardom may hinge on having role models and mentors who impart the right lessons. You can't choose your child's role models, but you can influence that choice by being a splendid role model yourself and encouraging them to seek others who share your values and determination.

Often, children's first role models are their school peers. As you know, the "cool" kids can also be the ones who drink, use drugs and get into trouble. In order to prevent your children from making them their role models, start talking about the qualities that make a good role model. As I say throughout this book, communication is *everything*. Respect your children's intelligence and talk, talk, talk as much as you can.

Children enjoy hearing about their parents' pasts. Talk openly about your childhood, what you did, what you saw and what happened. Talk about who your role models were when you were a child, how you saw the world then, how you felt about the world when you were your children's age. Who did you want to be? Are you the person you wanted to be? Are you somebody else? What made you who you are? What do you still hope to achieve, and how are you going to get there? Let your child know that it's OK not to have achieved every goal yet as long as you have a plan for reaching your next goal.

Nilou and I always talked about people who thought big, created big things for the world, made a difference, innovated, and are influencing our lives today. We tried to understand those people's lives and what we could learn from them. This is a great way to introduce your superstar to the idea of personal achievement and determination: make discussion a part of your routine. After every party or family gathering, we would sit together before going to bed and talk about what we learned from each person at the party. We talked about the loving grandma or how well-read so-and-so was. We talked about how we didn't want to be like the person who was so negative, and how we could be more positive like another guest. Nilou remembers our talks as far back as first grade and how learning in every occasion helped her become who she is now.

If your kids are anything like my daughter, they'll start firing off questions to you at high speed. Answer them, and then it's your turn. Ask who *their* role models are. They may talk about the popular kids at school, but they may also surprise you. Start talking about adults, pioneers who have done great things, or people they know and admire. Ask your child, "What makes these people special?" Talk about those who have achieved and those who have made a difference in the world. This person can be anyone from science, politics, arts, or economics, or can be someone from your family or neighborhood who has done something to make your smaller world a brighter place.

Have your kids research these extraordinary people. If they are people in the community, have your children talk to them and ask them to tell their story. If they are famous, global figures, try biographical books or Biography Channel DVDs. Get the book and read it together, or have your child read the book and discuss it with them. Watch the films together and talk about the people who inspired them.

Did these people like their childhood? Were they popular kids? Many superstars are those who were not very popular in school because they defied the norm. They were not cool. They have been loners. Maybe they were nerds. Teach your child what these people have in common is a vision and a commitment to making it real. That is the lesson they must learn.

Be Your Child's Role Model

If you want to have good kids, become a good adult. If you want your children to love people, love people yourself. If you want your children to be polite, be polite. If you want your children to be go-getters, be a go-getter. If you want your child to care for humanity, care for humanity. Your children will become who you show them they can become through your actions. Your words are important, but they pale before your actions. You should always be your child's greatest role model.

Who Were Your Role Models?

In the spaces below, write down the name of a role model who inspired you when you were your child's age. Then, next to his or her name, write down what about the person was such an inspiration to you. When your list is done, share it with your child and talk about each of these people. Finally, ask your child to create his or her own list.

Name	Reason

Start new activities. It doesn't matter if you are thirty, forty, fifty or sixty years old. Start a new sport, a new hobby, a new musical instrument, or a volunteer job. Go to seminars, learn new things, and get active. Become a bigger person and your children will learn from you.

When I called to confirm that Nilou had been accepted to the leadership camp, the lady on the phone who was in charge of the organization answered the line and said, "I really would like to meet you. In fact, the entire committee would." I asked her why. She said, "The essay your daughter wrote about you was so impressive, we all want to see who you are!" I was shocked. She had written about me! As part of the admission requirements, the girls were asked to write about a woman who had impressed them by being a leader or making a difference in the world. Nilou wrote about me.

If you have teenagers, you'll know what life was like at home. My teenage daughter and I fought all the time. There were times when she was a monster I felt I could barely tolerate. But this...this was something I was not prepared for. One morning, she came to my bedroom at 6:30, before I had gotten up to go to work, and said, "Mom, I have something I want to read to you." She read me her essay, which I've reprinted here:

> *I am proud to be the only daughter of Terri, the most admirable person in the world. Involving a great deal of effort, energy, persistence, and time, my wonderful mother has raised me with massive love and care. I respect how, when I was little, my mother, as a single parent, managed to raise me, work,*

and earn a master's degree as well. In addition to admiring and respecting her, I also learn from my mom. She's taught me so much, such as goal setting, following through, not giving up/quitting, fighting for my beliefs, about ethics, to love my family in Iran (even though they are thousands of miles away), to be positive, to be proactive, to have principles; how to make smart decisions, to set priorities, to first seek to understand, then be understood, to begin with the end in mind, how to improve my relationships with friends, to respect others, and how to be a leader. I have learned almost everything from my mother.

My mother inspires me to do positive things in my life. While trying to squeeze the best out of me, she's always helping me find the right direction. Her expectations of me are high, but with effort and work always achievable. Educating me with her knowledge of time management and how to find a balance between school, work, friends, and everything else, she has helped me be organized and on time with my activities. My thankfulness for having a mother that is as inspiring and admirable as mine is so immense that I don't know how I could ever repay her.

I cried that day and for days afterward. I was so touched by what she wrote about me -- how she thought about me. It made everything I had gone through in Germany and the U.S. worthwhile.

To myself, I was just a single mom. I had to take care of us, to get my university education while I raised my child and worked, too. But to Nilou, these were big, important things.

She looked at everybody else -- married people with two household incomes or divorced parents where one is at least helping financially; then she looked at us -- where her father didn't even know where we lived, and how I managed not only to keep a roof over our heads but tried to make her life exciting and exceptional. To me, that was just life, but to her, it made me her role model. I have never been prouder of anything.

She saw how other mothers would complain that they had "sacrificed everything for their children." We would roll our eyes at each other and think, "Get over it." I did everything for Nilou and myself at the same time and enjoyed it. I never felt that I sacrificed my life for my child. I lived it *with* her, and it was wonderful.

Confidence

Building confidence in your children starts with accepting and believing in them and teaching them to believe in themselves. This can start simply; if they bring home an art piece or some other creation that they made for you in school, if they sing a little song, if they pick a little daisy for you…make a big deal out of it. Praise them, thank them, appreciate them, make them feel like a star, and make them feel like they have great talent.

Never ever make fun of your children and do not allow them to make fun of others. It only takes a bit of disapproval from a parent to turn a child's fragile interest in painting or music into embarrassment. Being made fun of turns children into shy young adults. I have seen the direct relationship between children who were made fun of and those who were not, and the results clearly support this theory. I never allowed anybody to make fun of Nilou even if it was a joke. I made it clear to those adults whose sense of humor was mixed with put-downs that such comments were unacceptable in my home. I also didn't allow her to make fun of others.

Plentiful praise lets your children know they are doing something right, so they will become self-confident. I cheered Nilou on in everything that she did and it was the right thing to do. I also always watched for the fine line between giving her confidence and building her arrogance. Of course, you also have to avoid undeserved praise under the guise of "boosting self-esteem." You don't want to give children empty praise when they don't put forth effort or have a bad attitude. They will quickly learn to do the minimum. But when they try their hardest and do something with total enthusiasm and effort, no matter what the result is, they deserve your complete approval. Go to all ends to give praise and appreciation to your children's actions – if they do something that you want to see your children repeat and do better.

I always taught Nilou to give compliments to others and see the greatness in others, rather than worry about receiving compliments from them. I always told her, "If you know you are good, you don't need to speak highly of yourself. If you believe in yourself there is no need for self-praise and arrogance." I told her not to boast or show off, but rather let others discover her wonderful qualities for themselves. When she crossed the line into boasting as a young child, I always stopped her short and reminded her that she should never see herself as better / or higher than any other person.

Truly confident people become more likable when they are down to earth. Teach the philosophy of humility to your child. Teach them to be modest, kind, giving and strong. A truly confident person who is also truly humble will shine much more than an arrogant, scared person! Confident people have no need for shows of ego or vanity. Only insecure people need to bolster their weak self-esteem with continual "Look how wonderful I am" displays.

Independence

> *Your children are not your children. They are the sons and daughters of Life's longing for itself. They came through you but not from you and though they are with you yet they belong not to you.*
>
> — *Kahlil Gibran*

I didn't have a choice but to teach Nilou to be independent early. Even if you have a choice and could do everything for your children, don't. Your number one job as a parent is to make it so your children do not need you -- to make them independent human beings capable of thriving on their own in the world.

Learning independence for Nilou started when she was not even three years old, when she learned to tie her shoes. She had to do it because we had to work together to get her to school and me to work or a university class. I figured teaching her to tie her shoes as early as age three would help us get ready faster. This was out of necessity. If you work, run a household, go to school, and raise a child, you come up with creative ideas to get things done faster. Even if you are not a single parent and you have all the time in the world, it's worth it to teach your kids this kind of skill. You teach them the alphabet, colors, numbers, and so many other things -- why not teach them independence too?

I have seen mothers who help their children dress at the age of seven or eight. These mothers habitually hover over their children, doing everything for them because they feel it makes them better mothers. But in reality, they are crippling their kids. If you do everything for a child, naturally the child will fall back on that support. I have found that mothers who dress and feed their older children are really self-serving; they are trying to keep their little ones little for as long as possible. They have made themselves more important than their children.

Healthy children should *want* to do things on their own. That's what the "terrible twos" are about: children discovering and asserting their independence. I motivated Nilou and excited her into liking the idea of doing things by herself. It got to the point that she wouldn't let me do anything anymore.

Independent in School

School is every child's first taste of scary independence; there is nothing quite as painful for parents as leaving their child at nursery school for the first time and watching them cry and panic as Mom or Dad drive away. You are their whole world and they are frightened without you. But the same thing always happens: within a few days, scared, weeping children start playing and making friends, and after a short while you can't get them to *leave* nursery school. This is as it should be.

When they start elementary school some children need a little help, but after a short time they have to learn to do their homework independently. If you need to be there and check on everything they do, you are making a mistake. Teach them to do their homework on their own, raise them with passion and joy about school and school work; don't do their homework with them. Independent children can become confident adults easier than others, because they know their way around and they can take care of themselves.

Living in Europe allowed Nilou to use public transportation and get around safely to and from school. She was only in fourth grade when she learned to take the bus and go to her piano and her jazz dance lessons. It is not as easy in the U.S., but there are always ways. Most public schools provide buses immediately after school and later in the day as well. Nilou learned to not need transportation; nor did she need me to watch all her athletic events and activities. She didn't need my approval to motivate her to do her best. I praised her when she was with me and when she told me about things she did.

I forced Nilou to become her own person very early on, in part because I had no choice, but also because I knew it would make her stronger, more self-reliant and more confident. As a very young girl, she traveled by herself. She learned how to adapt and stay safe abroad. She was a teenager when she visited places like Spain, Switzerland, and France by herself. Later, during her first years of college, she independently traveled to South Africa to run the Two Ocean Marathon and studied in South America. This was all part of her maturing into the person she has become. If I had been fearful and traveled with her to look over her shoulder every time, she would not have developed the skills she has today.

If you want to have independent and confident children, let them take care of themselves. Don't baby them even if you have all the time in the world and you really ache to make things easier for them. Life will be more difficult for them later. Be strong, be the grownup, and show them you love them, not by doing everything for them, but by letting them learn, make their own mistakes, and become independent people.

CHAPTER TWO:
School and the Superstar

A school is not a factory. Its raison d'être is to provide opportunity for experience.

      —*J.L. Carr, British novelist*

I assume you think of school and grades as one of your highest priorities as a parent. So do I. Education is very important. The question is, how important? How much should we push our children to go for the highest grades possible? When does pushing become harmful?

Some people think their children have to be good in every subject and keep straight A's all the way to the end of high school and college. Is that you? Let me ask you this: Were you good at everything? Really? You got A grades in every subject you tried? Well, bravo for you. Now forget about it. Your child is not you. He or she doesn't have to be excellent in every subject. What matters is that they work hard and enjoy the process of learning. Rather than pushing them, sometimes we need to encourage them to enjoy learning and discovery.

Like you, I was worried about what was going to happen to my child in school. She was good in every class in elementary school. So good, she was mostly bored. She got into trouble because she learned quickly and her elementary school teacher in Germany taught in a way that didn't stimulate her. So she started to rebel and act out. When she went to middle school, things started to change. This was a greater challenge with more interesting subjects and advanced classes. She started to learn English and get busy with more serious studies. The discipline calls stopped and she was on her way to a love affair with academia.

Enjoying School

In our house the meaning of the school was painted in vibrant, energetic colors. School was a great place to be in; it was a fun place to go to. It was a place where one can learn interesting things for life and enjoy the process of learning. I planted the seed in her mind early on and nourished it as she grew up. Unlike most children, Nilou liked Mondays; she liked the end of holidays and the end of the summer. She looked forward to going back to school, no matter how much fun we had during the summer. She had love and passion for school. This was the culture in my parents' house and I brought it over to my house for Nilou when I became a parent. It is an easy thing to do if you start early enough, and it makes parenting a lot easier if your children go to school with eagerness and joy everyday.

In high school, Nilou was in all Advanced Placement (AP) classes, and for those classes where the International Baccalaureate (IB) program was offered, she was in the IB classes. I recommend IB classes wherever they are available. They are generally more challenging than AP programs, and some colleges give more weight to them in admissions as well as more class credit. It was a good program to keep her busy, push her to excel, and prepare her for the demands of college. I was very proud of her.

But even as all this was going on, I was careful not to let school replace every other activity in our lives. Even though academics were very important to me, they never meant everything. Children need to be involved in different things while they work on their formal education. A well-rounded child does better in life.

In high school, Nilou was not the best in every subject but she did her best at everything. I encouraged her to focus on those fields that she loved and was good at. She loved history and learning about the world. I encouraged her to do her best in the subjects that she loved. Don't get me wrong; I never would suggest giving your children permission to do poorly at any subject. Help them choose what they really enjoy, what they are good at, and what will best serve them to build on in life. Encourage them to try their best in the subjects in which they need to improve. The important thing is to keep your children motivated and enthusiastic about school and learning.

Though IB physics was tough for Nilou, she still enjoyed the subject and went to her teacher, Mr. Book (a perfect teacher's name) every day for help. She maintained a positive attitude throughout high school, which had a great deal to do with positive reinforcement at home.

Education is the passport to the future, for tomorrow belongs to those who prepare for it today.
— *Malcolm X*

Find out what your child's favorite subject is. All children have one. Discover what it is and help them be stars at it. With the subjects they don't enjoy or struggle with, help them build on their strengths. Do not overemphasize their weakness. Encourage them to take certain classes because it will help them directly or indirectly in college and in different areas of their lives. Children have a natural curiosity. Incite this curiosity in them, particularly in subjects in which they don't excel. Ask them how these subjects relate to real life. When Nilou was frustrated with a physics assignment, I asked her this and we talked about it. She replied that physics could be tangible because she could relate motion, friction, and other areas of the science to everyday life. She said when she broke a dish she could think about its particles getting displaced and be able to calculate the measurements. When we drove off a ramp on the highway in the rain, she could think about the decreased friction and therefore need for decreased speed to go around the curve. I helped her train herself to find a way to like even the subjects that were not her favorites but that she needed to learn. This kept her engaged.

Homework

Homework is a test of discipline, and it starts at an early age. The more you help your children with their homework, the worse off they are. The more you let your children do their homework on their own and be independent, the more you help them.

You should not need to help your children do their homework, even in elementary school. If they have questions, they can come to you and ask. But do not look over their shoulders and do the work for them. You will make them dependent upon you. Super stars are not spoon-fed. They learn to be independent early.

Left to figure out their homework on their own, they might get into some trouble at first. They'll survive, and they will learn after that. Remember, you won't be there to push them when they are in college. Remind them of homework, of course, and insist that it gets done on time. Middle and high school children don't need mom and dad's help with academics; they need a mom and dad to talk with and a support network to lean on.

If they are weak in one field and need tutoring, that is a different story. You might want to have someone come and help them after school. But that should be the end of your involvement. There is enough help in school, after school and before school for them to use. They can ask for help from teachers or classmates. Help them develop initiative.

Homework is an essential tool for teaching your child discipline and consistent effort. Make it a priority; they cannot play on weeknights or participate in any weekend activities until all homework is complete. They will complain, but by standing firm you do them a huge favor. Tell them about the fun plans you have for the weekend or the afternoon and let them know that, until homework is done, nothing will happen. You'll be amazed how quickly assignments get completed! This is the way to encourage discipline and a strong work ethic; this is how it worked in our house. No two hours of TV each night. Homework was first and homework got done.

Working Fosters Appreciation

Should a child be expected to work and earn money while in school? A thousand times yes. I strongly believe that every child has to work to earn money and become responsible. It helps their financial life and it builds confidence. Yet some parents worry that their children will be distracted by work from their studies, will burn out, or will place a higher value on money than on education.

I disagree. If children work to earn their dollars, they appreciate the dollars that come into their hands and they become more responsible adults. If they start working and learn to handle workplace issues before they have real job responsibility, they have it much easier in their career. They learn how to get along with co-workers and fulfill their work responsibilities, and they learn how to handle problems while they are young.

CHAPTER 2 - SCHOOL AND THE SUPERSTAR

You give a gift to your children when you encourage them to earn their own money and maybe even to save or invest for their future. It doesn't matter what neighborhood you live in and how wealthy or poor your neighbors are. If you send your children to work, you do more than teaching them about the value of money. You teach them to develop work ethic which will serve them better in life than almost any other lesson.

I love the example of Tony Robbins. Even though he was a famous speaker, a self-help author and multi-millionaire by the time his daughter turned sixteen, he told her she could not have a car for her birthday unless she earned enough money to pay for half of it. She was upset about this, but she did the work and earned the money, and when she did her part, her father matched it and she bought her car. That is a wonderful lesson in hard work and in not having a sense of entitlement. I have seen many wealthy families do exactly that to teach their kids responsibility, self-reliance, and appreciation.

Nilou's first job was babysitting during middle school. In high school she worked in the school library, at a community center, in a law firm, for a DJ company, at Hallmark, at flower shop, as a personal trainer at a gym, and at a restaurant, where she was fired because she spilled soup on someone and dropped plates in the kitchen. She learned life lessons and earned her dollars. She participated in school activities, athletics, did volunteer work and worked for her pocket money. She didn't burn out and her grades didn't suffer. She learned to work for her dreams; and she learned that they would not be handed to her. She became truly appreciative, an important lesson.

Encourage your children to work to earn money. Let them do babysitting, mow lawns, work for the store around the corner, sell lemonade, or sell things on eBay. Get creative and help them become productive. If they have an entrepreneurial mind, support their ideas. It doesn't matter what the idea is -- help it blossom.

Heidi and Andy

Andy and Heidi have a twelve-year-old daughter and nine-year-old twin boys. They have used creative ways to make their children responsible, independent and well-rounded. Andy retired in his early forties and took his family on an around-the-world trip for nine months. They home schooled their children and brought the greatest memories back home. Their children are rich in the experiences they gained during that nine months. Heidi and Andy have gone even further to ensure their children are hard-working and independent. The children don't get an allowance. They work and get paid for the help they provide their parents. To get paid, they have to invoice their parents! When they want to buy things, they use their own money. Their parents will lend them money, but the children must keep track of the amount and make regular payments until they pay off their debts.

Recently, they started to ask the kids to watch themselves without a babysitter. Heidi's father lives next door in case something happens, but it never has. Each child is responsible for him/herself and gets one dollar per hour for self-babysitting. Kelsey was eleven and the boys were eight when they started this.

Most impressive to me, every year on their birthday, the children take a new responsibility. For example:

- When they were six years old, they were charged with opening the door and welcoming guests. At the same age, they were expected to rise from their seats for older people and women. They learned pleasant manners and social skills early.

- At age seven, they had to empty the trashcans and take the trash out.

- At age eight, they started giving to charity and investing their money. Each child gives a percentage of their money to the poor every time they earn anything: they save eighty percent, give ten percent to others and have the remaining ten percent for fun.

- At age nine, the new responsibility was making their own lunches for school.

- When they turn ten, they must start doing their own laundry.

When Kelsey wanted a horse, she helped build the barn and paint it. She earned the money to buy her horse by working. Children should not get what they want just because. They have to work and wait for what they want. Furthermore, in Heidi and Andy's family, not all jobs are paid; they are expected. Mowing the lawn is an obligation, not a job. The children are responsible for putting their dishes in the dishwasher and bringing in the groceries, and they don't receive a penny for that work.

I love Heidi and Andy's ideas and encourage all parents to emulate them. What jobs can you give your children to make money before you can send them out to earn money and before they are old enough to be hired outside of your house? How about painting fences and buildings, digging dirt for landscaping, or washing the car? Be creative.

Work, Not Talent, Brings Out Genius

Many people like to say some children are simply talented, as if that's enough to succeed. They either have it or they don't. They see gifted children and assume they will automatically do well in whatever pursuit they choose, period. They don't realize children only want to do what they enjoy. Beyond that, they need to develop strong work habits and wide interests if they are to be successful in life.

There are always ways to bring out a child's multiple interests and encourage them to work at something even if you think they don't have natural gifts. We always appreciate what we struggle for. Your job is to find the brilliance and genius in your child and, like a good gardener, bring it out.

I helped Nilou develop skills in many different directions. She speaks five languages because language is a learnable skill. She runs marathons and ultra marathons because running is a learnable skill…and because she did not make it onto any other teams in school. That is not athletic talent. It is determination. Nilou loves to dance and is a great dancer. She started by watching people dance, then came up with new dance moves, and choreographed dances for herself and her friends. She plays piano a little bit, and she likes to paint and create her own artwork because it makes her feel good, but she won't make any money at any of these things. That's not the point. The point is in helping your children develop skills and interests in different areas and encouraging them to live with passion.

When Nilou was young I had her in activities before kindergarten: ballet, piano, jazz, tennis, basketball, painting, you name it. She was not particularly great at anything. But she was my star and I was not disappointed. I was hoping to find something that she would love and I was going in the right direction. My role was keeping her motivated and excited about all these activities until we found the right thing for her. I knew she would finally focus on one thing that was right for her, but in the meantime she would learn many different things. In helping Nilou get a taste of many different aspects of life, I was keeping her happy and healthy and out of trouble. I was training her athletically, emotionally, culturally, and socially. You don't need a super genius to raise a superstar. Neither do you need a great deal of money. If you have money and your child is talented, then you are lucky. If neither is true, not to worry. There are always inexpensive options, and you never know when that activity that captures your child's imagination and brings out their latent gifts will come along.

I remember, when Nilou first started running, she only had one pair of running shorts. Other students had a variety of running outfits, but she knew she would have to be patient. She knew she would get some running gear for Christmas, for her birthday, and on other occasions. I would not buy things for her until she proved to me that she would stick with the activity. Once she proved she was a dedicated runner, I was right behind her.

Encourage, motivate and cheer your children and tell them they are wonderful. Keep them busy. Your child will learn both things that they are good at and skills that they will use throughout their lives.

As a result of all her activities, Nilou became a hard worker with a passion and interest in many different things. Today, her brain and body are trained to learn everything she wants to learn. She has a powerful interest in new things. This is not talent; she needs just as much time as anyone else when she starts learning something new. It is all about a good training, a work ethic and a disciplined mind.

There is genius in every child; what brings it out is relentless work and encouragement. You can turn any child to a superstar if you follow the formula. Our purpose is to create a world of caring, loving, happy, healthy, well-rounded and super successful individuals -- not just sports gurus or rich people who are never fulfilled in life.

Battling Peer Pressure

We all are pressured by our peers and by people who surround us. Children, who are still developing a sense of identity, are especially vulnerable to this. Your response? Help them choose better peers and get them involved in healthy activities with healthy peers. The friendships and connections that your children make during and after school are the most critical factors shaping them into superstars, losers, or average adults. Some studies suggest that we become the average of the ten closest people to us. You *need* to know who your children are friends with!

When Nilou was in school, many people asked me how I kept her healthy and active. My answer: "I watch who her friends are." I put the brakes on some of her friendships and I promoted others. Even if it meant her being alone for awhile, I didn't let her spend much time with the wrong friends. This might sound too controlling, but it is a parent's responsibility to show the judgment in people their children cannot. I didn't allow her to be with those children who could be a negative influence on her. I limited and directed her friendships. I had long conversations with her about the harm of some friendships and the benefit of others.

We had arguments and sometimes reasoning on why a friendship was good or not. There were times that she wanted to help other kids. She wanted to be a savior to some of the worst children in school. While I respected her desire to help, she could not see the danger that she could fall into: the same trap as the troubled kids, if she got too close. My suggestion was that she gets involved in formal school activities designed to help at-risk kids...not become friends with them. I told her she would become like people she would hang out with and I refused to let her choose the wrong ones.

Choosing Friends

One of the wisest moves I made with my daughter was to give her a system for choosing her friends: her friends had to be better than her in at least one major area of life. She still uses this lesson in her daily life. Her friends all have something that she wants to learn from. To become her friends, they had to prove that they could teach her something and be a good influence. She also was supposed to teach them something and be a valuable friend for them. She and her friends had to learn and be inspired by each other. I would not support average friendships with average children. My philosophy was: we love everyone and are good to our community, but when it comes to choosing friends we become very selective.

Another smart way for keeping children out of trouble is to get them involved in activities that work against negative peer pressure. Nilou was in middle school when I found out about the "Power Team" in her school. Members learned to become community leaders in the fight against drugs and alcohol. They learned to handle peer pressure and various learned ways of saying "no" to drugs and alcohol, and they learned to teach other children how to do the same. They periodically visited other schools and promoted an anti-drug and alcohol life for younger children. To be a member, you had to never try drugs, alcohol or cigarettes. The students in the Power Team were leaders. They would talk to other children to make them aware of the dangers of drugs and alcohol, or being influenced by peer pressure into making big mistakes. This was a great way for Nilou to stay involved in healthy activities and away from trouble. Her feeling of usefulness and purpose was something she would not exchange for any drug or alcohol offer from friends.

Build confidence in your children to help them with peer pressure, keep them away from drugs and alcohol, surround them with good friends, get them involved in community leadership, and you will raise confident children who are not pressured by the wrong peers. Keep your children busy in healthy activities and sports. Share with them the joys of work and money well-earned and the pleasure of overcoming weaknesses to excel at something they thought they could not achieve. You'll keep them focused, healthy, happy, and teach them discipline that will serve them wherever life takes them.

CHAPTER THREE:
Superstar Habits for Life

Good habits formed at youth make all the difference.
—Aristotle

Our habits define who we are and who we become. How is this possible? Think about the daily things you do by routine and how they shape your life. You exercise, eat, speak to others and work based on habitual patterns you have developed over years. If you know a person's habits, you will probably have a good idea what he or she will be capable of in life. Small things that we do every day have, over years and decades, the power to determine our futures. If you eat right and exercise a little each day, you are more likely to be lean and healthy in your old age. If you smoke and eat high-fat foods, you are more likely to be obese, have heart problems and be limited in what you can do later in life. It is really this simple: we are our habits.

When you are raising a superstar child, it is essential to instill good, healthy and productive habits early in life. It is so much easier to get children to eat right and exercise when they are five years old than to try and change bad habits when they are seventeen!

Aristotle said, *"We are what we repeatedly do. Excellence, therefore, is not an act, but a habit."* Life habits are everything we teach our children, from taking care of their body and soul to having proper manners and behaving well in groups. Some learn these things as children, some learn it later, and some never learn. Give the gift of good habits to your children early and make life easier for them.

This chapter looks at some of the most important habits I have worked to develop in my daughter—habits that I believe have become the foundation for the happiness and fulfillment she experiences today. I hope with my easy-to-follow techniques and examples I can help you raise your superstars with positive lifelong habits.

Eating Habits for life

Today's consumer culture has produced a galaxy of foods filled with ingredients that have never existed in nature. This has warped our sense of taste so badly that many children in America cannot even tell what a raw strawberry tastes like because they are so accustomed to chemical simulations. You can see where this is going: teach your children to eat natural, simple, fresh and healthy foods. It is one of the most important habits you can impart to them.

It is shocking to read food labels in the U.S. and see how much sugar, sodium, saturated fat, and chemicals are in everything. Furthermore, a food might say it is "organic" on the box, but that may mean it contains one organic ingredient while the rest of the box is filled with processed foods and chemicals. Follow this general rule: the fresher the food, the better. Stay away from so-called "convenience" foods packed with empty calories and salt. The less a food has been modified by the time it reaches your table, chances are the healthier it is for you and your child.

Help your children get used to eating healthy food, fresh vegetables and fresh fruit. Look for local organic produce and find a farmer's market in or near your town. Keep your kids away from junk food, canned food and processed packaged snacks. It is not hard to develop the habit of loving fresh fruits and vegetables if you start early enough and educate your children about the importance of healthy nutrition. A healthier diet has another benefit as well: it is usually cheaper than fast food and processed food.

Exercise

Write down everything you ate and drank in the last three days. Then write down everything you gave your children to eat during the same time.

_____
_____
_____
_____

_____
_____
_____
_____
_____
_____
_____
_____
_____
_____

How much alike are your lists? How much of what your child ate was fresh? How much of it was junk food, "dead" processed food, or food dripping with fat, salt or sugar? A healthy diet should consist of about seventy percent fresh fruits and vegetables; in other words, live food. The rest of your diet should contain raw nuts, beans and whole grains. How did you do on your test? Is your diet close to being healthy, or do you need to review your own eating habits first, and then help your children start eating healthy?

Your children will learn to eat what you eat. If they see you eating obesity-producing, high-fat junk foods, they will eat the same things. On the other hand, if they see you enjoying fruit salads as desserts, they will learn to love fresh fruit. You owe it to your children to adopt healthy eating habits yourself.

Ban Fast Food

Feeding your children fast food and heavily processed foods is not going to help them become healthy adults. You worked late? You are too busy to cook? Not acceptable excuses. There is *always* time to eat well. When I was raising Nilou, I had to work, study, do the grocery shopping, clean the house, do the laundry and much more. I had to think ahead about how to provide fresh, healthy foods on the table at mealtime and for snacks.

Salad and fresh fruit were always part of our daily diet. Nilou cannot live without salad these days. If she doesn't eat salad and fresh vegetables for a day or two, she gets insatiable cravings; if she is traveling she will go on a relentless hunt for a salad bar. I would do fast, easy things to encourage good eating, like cut up mixed fruits as an afternoon snack and take it to her room while she was studying. We hardly ever had soda in our home. Instead, we drank water and fresh juices. Thanks to all this healthy nutrition that began when she was small, Nilou hardly ever gets sick or gets a cold or the flu; her immune system is immensely strong. She never missed a day of school in twelve years for being sick, and hasn't missed a day of college, either.

Start yourself and your children on healthy eating habits and good nutrition. Stop going to fast food places. They are havens of unhealthy calories, high cholesterol, and high saturated fat. Don't kid yourself that you are doing right when you serve canned vegetables, either. They have many of the vital nutrients leached out of them by processing. Instead, add salad, fresh fruits and vegetables to your daily diet. Train your children to eat—and love—fresh foods served as naturally as possible.

One more tip: teach your child to garden and learn where food comes from. Nothing is better than eating something from your own yard that you grew with your own hands. If you don't have a yard, grow herbs and vegetables in pots; we did that on our balcony. You always know it's free of chemicals and pesticides!

Sports and Exercise

Physical activity has always been part of my daughter's life. Sports and exercise were something that she simply had to do. As a child I was never encouraged to participate in sports by my parents, and I wanted Nilou to have the benefits I didn't enjoy. I started her in ballet and tennis; she then switched over to jazz dance, progressed to judo lessons, and later tried gymnastics. In high school, she tried out for the field hockey team and basketball team, but she was cut before the end of tryouts each time. Fortunately and unfortunately, she was not very good at any of these activities. I say "fortunately and unfortunately" because even though not doing well was hard on her, it kept her motivated to find something she was good at and would enjoy.

That something was running. Running was her last resort, but it became the sports in which she continues to shine. She fell in love with running quickly. When children find the right activity, and you have planted the seeds of optimism, determination, and persistence in them, they simply go for it on their own. When she started running track and cross-country, she loved it immediately. I wanted her to do something for her health and fitness, but I never thought it would be running.

She was not very good at the beginning, but she trained hard, stayed after practice to run laps and improve her speed, and made varsity by her junior year in high school. Eventually, she became the captain of her cross-country, winter track, and spring track teams. She became a "track addict" who loved to go to practice every day. This is a good example of what I have already discussed: help your children discover what they love and they will shine. There is something that every child can be good at and will love.

Today, Nilou has run twelve marathons and ultra-marathons worldwide. She is planning to run at least one marathon on every continent (including Antarctica) by the time she is twenty-seven. She talks about the North Pole marathon, one of the world's most difficult races (run on the ice sheet in the most difficult weather conditions), and she plans to participate in an Ironman triathlon in the near future.

The benefits of running went far beyond the dirt of the track. Running improved her focus and concentration. I could see how much better her schoolwork was after her long runs. To this day, she relies on the oxygenation of a long run to get her thoughts flowing and her mind racing to work on an academic challenge. She even goes for a long run before her law school exams or when she is preparing for important papers.

Being There for Every Game?

Having a child in sports brings up another issue for parents: should you go to every game or meet? Should you feel guilty if you cannot go? I was always there when Nilou needed support, but I couldn't see the point of going to every single track meet. She knew I had to work. Instead, I taught my daughter to cheer for herself. She was so independent, because of how she had been raised, that she didn't need the motivation of a family cheering section to try her best.

Watching your children's every game is not the way to motivate them. In the summer of 2005, Nilou and I joined my sister to watch my niece's soccer game. The scene was like something out of a bad sitcom: parents sitting in the heat, mostly overweight and unhealthy, eating hot dogs and junk food. Most of them didn't look like they had ever set foot inside a gym, yet they were hoping their children would develop different habits. Since children learn from watching their parents, that is unlikely.

I asked my sister why she came to her daughter's game when she was so exhausted. She said she did it because all the other mothers or fathers were doing it, and she didn't want her daughter to feel bad because all the other parents were there. Translation: she did it because she would have felt guilty if she had not attended. Guilt is a bad reason to give time to your children.

Nilou and I had a long conversation after that day. She said the reason she was so serious about her running and triathlons in college was because she believed sports was something she was doing for herself, not for me. She said she did it because I taught her the importance of sports and exercise for life. She thanked me for not spoiling her and not watching all her races, and for helping her become independent instead of depending on my praise to motivate her to do her best. She did her best for *herself.*

You want to do your children a favor? Teach them to cheer for themselves, pursue their goals and persist. Let them know you are proud of them even if you are not present at every game. Go to their games every couple of months or once a quarter, but not every weekend. Give them the assurance of love and recognition without your physical presence at every game. Who cares what other parents think? Supporting your children is about quality time, not being there out of a sense of obligation or guilt.

Recently, I was talking to a friend who was worried about her daughter, who was stressed out and getting sick because of all her schoolwork and activities. She told me that a couple of days before, her daughter went to her ballet class after missing it for several weeks and came home relaxed, shining, and happy. She got over her illness and her homework even improved. Such is the power that a beloved activity has over children. Encourage your children to find a sport or physical activity they can love and can give it everything they have. If you want them to be fulfilled and balanced, motivate them to exercise and take care of their body while they do everything else for their lives. Their bodies and minds will benefit.

Respect and Proper Manners

Clean up after yourself, put your dish in the dishwasher, be respectful to adults, don't talk to your mom and dad like you talk with your classmates, respect your grandparents, when you stay at someone's house make your own bed and don't expect them to clean up after you, knock before you enter…

Each of these life habits can be instilled from early childhood. Each is about respect and proper manners for life. Respect is a vital lesson that children should take into their adulthood, and it cuts two ways: respect for others and respect for themselves. Respect starts at home. The day you make your children pick up their own trash and not leave it for you to take care of, you begin teaching it. The day you teach them to get up and give their seat to a disabled or elderly person, the lesson continues. The day that grandma comes in and they know they are not supposed to lie down in front of TV, the lesson takes root.

Nilou knew she had to get up and give her seat to an adult by the time she was six years old. Respect and manners are habits that must be taught. By the time Nilou was in first grade, I didn't have to say anything. Politeness was a habit. She knew that she always had to sit in the back seat when there was an adult in the car. We never needed to discuss the issue or negotiate. These are very basic behaviors I encourage you to begin teaching your child early.

As you plant the seeds of politeness, respect, and proper manners in your children, you are helping them grow into adults with the ability to encourage goodwill, lead others and radiate positive energy. You help them be happy with themselves and with others, and other people will feel better being around your children. What is better than raising children who feel great about themselves and make others feel wonderful and worthwhile as well?

Books and Reading

Reading should begin long before children start elementary school. Many parents read to their children when they are as young as three months old, and I encourage this. Infants may not understand the words, but they learn what a book is, how the pages are turned, how a story is organized, and so on. Children hear more than we realize, and early reading exposes them to the wonder and poetry of language. You can even read to them in a language other than the one you speak daily at home! Let them savor the sounds and phrases of many tongues.

Problems with reading arise in elementary school. Once they are in school, kids start reading schoolbooks for their homework. This is usually when the parental ball is dropped. If reading becomes part of homework and nothing else, before you know it reading is a chore. Reading should be a joy for your kids.

The longer you wait to start a child on developing good reading habits, the tougher it becomes to make reading a part of their daily lives. Pre-kindergarten kids fall in love with books easily; middle schoolers who didn't grow up reading find their affections tempted by video games, time with friends, movies and yes, the opposite sex. Starting early is essential if you want to start an affair between your child and the written word that will last a lifetime.

Unfortunately, not all parents abide by this wisdom. I have seen children with straight-A grades who have never read a book outside of schoolwork. That is an indication of a mind going slack and lazy, especially if reading is replaced at home by videogames, television, and the Internet. Children who only read out of obligation learn to memorize, but they don't develop the creative thinking and problem solving skills that are essential to success as an adult. A superstar child is well-read outside of school—novels, biographies, non-fiction, history and much more.

School alone will not make a child a knowledgeable and well-rounded person. Schools teach the basics. But you are the most important teaching influence in your child's life; it is your responsibility to provide the majority of your child's education that your school cannot possibly provide. You must help your children develop important qualities like imagination and leadership skills—encourage them, push them and do everything possible to get them in the habit of reading books in different areas.

This is not rocket science. Make reading a family activity. Instead of watching TV after dinner, huddle on the couch as a family and read books together, everyone with their own age-appropriate book. Look into biographies or autobiographies that your child can understand. Even fantasy and science fiction books are fine, as they encourage imagination and teach story structure and metaphor.

Take your list to the bookstore or the library, get the books and sit together on a Friday night or whenever you have your family time. Talk about the importance of reading books. Show them all the books that you now brought home and explain this is going to be a family activity you are sure they will enjoy. Suggest that everyone read one book and then discuss them as a family. This turns reading into sharing, and everyone learns something, even the parents.

Useful Tricks

Renowned motivational speaker, sales trainer and author Zig Ziglar talked about buying books that he knew were good for his children. He would tell them that if they read the book, summarized it, and shared what they learned, he would give them twenty dollars. After reading ten to fifteen books, his children didn't even want the money; they learned so much that they wanted to read more just because they loved it. The money was no longer important.

Set deadlines for finishing books. Don't leave it up to your children to finish on their own time, or you will be waiting a while. Explain to them that you want them to read a book in a week or a month, and in your next family meeting have them share what they learned by giving a summary of the book. This is excellent practice for a skill they can use in school.

By instilling reading habits early, you will raise well-rounded, educated children. Don't limit reading and education to school. Use the free time like summer breaks for readings that will change their lives.

Positive Thinking

We must have perseverance and above all confidence in ourselves. We must believe that we are gifted for something and that this thing must be attained.
—Marie Curie

Reading this book, you may be wondering how it was possible for me to go through everything I went through and stay sane. It was difficult, but not impossible. The key? Positive thinking! Through years of raising a child on my own without any support from her father, I went through a lot of emotional and financial ups and downs. The key to my survival was seeing the light at the end of the tunnels and finding a good reason for things that didn't seem so good when they were happening.

Nilou and I became emotional black belts at erasing bad experiences and memories, building on the good memories, and using the experiences as lessons toward a better future. We started fresh every day with positive energy and love for one another and everyone around us. We grew as a result of this habit. I became a better person as I was raising and teaching my daughter to learn positive thinking. I shared life lessons with her as I was learning them myself. At times, it was the only way to survive; other times it was more comforting. Teach your children to focus on the positive and stop their complaints! Remind yourself and your children regularly of all the things you have that you should appreciate.

Fear of Failure

Never, never, never, never give up.
— *Winston Churchill*

When Nilou was trying to decide what college to attend, she sent applications to some Ivy League schools; she didn't want to go anywhere that was less than great. But her SAT scores were not very good. Standardized tests have never been her strength. She was great at writing papers and had a fantastic GPA, but her testing skills left a lot to be desired.

Well, for better or worse, those tests are one of the most important parts of the application process for good schools. She didn't get into any of her top schools. Rejection after rejection filled the mailbox. She had only gotten into one school: her single backup college. She was sad and frustrated by this reversal, but she resigned herself to going to the backup university.

She started college life at American University in Washington, D.C. She made friends and started to believe that she was in a great place, particularly for studying international relations, the field of study she loved. She started saying she didn't want any more than what she had. This made me prick up my ears. This didn't sound like the go-getter I had raised!

We started having long talks, and I had to remind her of her dreams and goals— what she really wanted and what she was capable of doing. I told her she was getting too comfortable and that she was too scared to try and fail again. She disagreed with me, but it was clear I had struck a nerve. She loved studying international relations, and this was one of the best schools in the country for that field. She kept saying, "I am fine here, I have made friends, and I don't want to go anywhere else." I kept reminding her of her bigger goals, and finally the harsh truth came out. She had tears in her eyes as she said, "I don't want to fail again. I just want to stay here and not do anything more and not ever fail again. I don't want to experience those rejection letters any more."

Aha. Fear of failure was paralyzing my girl. We talked, discussed, discovered, and analyzed everything. Clearly, she was running scared of failing. I reminded her of my many failures in my career climb at United Airlines, in moving from country to country, and in having difficulties as an immigrant. I was living proof that failure is not fatal—that it can even be a springboard to greater things.

She started to open her eyes. She sent transfer applications to other schools. In the end, she got into the number-one school in her field and her choice, Georgetown University's School of Foreign Service. She continued studying international relations. She graduated magna cum laude in May 2006. We celebrated her persistence and hard work. She will never forget how much strength she needed to follow her dreams and get where she belonged.

It was not easy to get into the top international relations school in the country with mediocre SATs. How did she do it? She saw every person she could see, from professors to people at the admission office. She told them about her accomplishments, about the projects that she had worked on. She told them everything that she could do and how she would make the school proud to be able to claim her as an alumnus one day. She didn't give up.

I will never forget the day we received the letter. She went to the mailbox to get the mail. I drove the car out of the garage while she opened the envelope. Suddenly she was screaming, her eyes and mouth wide open, "Mom, I got into Georgetown!" I hugged her and we cried and screamed together. Persistence and belief had triumphed! She will never forget the strength she needed to follow her dreams and to get where she belonged. I believed in her until she learned to believe in herself.

Dangerously Positive

Some of Nilou's friends in college called her "dangerously positive." Sometimes they could not keep up with her positive energy. That is not an accident. Together, during the roughest of times, we trained ourselves to find at least one good reason for everything that happens in life. It's a fun way of living. It takes some practice, but then it becomes part of life. We watched the movie *The Secret* together and saw our lives in many of those examples. We had lived the "Law of Attraction" numerous times without having watched the movie. It is amazing how our life is shaped by what goes on in our mind.

Try this exercise with your children. In the space provided below, write about the times that you failed and got up afterwards. What were your biggest fears, when you thought the world was ending? How did you recover, regroup and make it anyway?

_____
_____
_____
_____
_____
_____
_____
_____
_____
_____

CHAPTER 3 - SUPERSTAR HABITS FOR LIFE

Talk with your children about your failures and how you responded to them. Talk about the times that you failed. Talk about the times that you dusted yourself off and tried again. Speak with them about the pain that you have gone through and the lessons that you learned. Talk to them when they get bad grades. Remind them that the only time they can fail is when they become negative and give up. Positive thinking becomes a lifelong habit that will help your children become superstars.

CHAPTER FOUR:
The Superstar Abroad

The more one does and sees and feels, the more one is able to do, and the more genuine may be one's appreciation of fundamental things like home, and love, and understanding of companionship.

—Amelia Earhart

Travel has been part of our lives since the beginning. Living in Europe made it possible to travel to many countries easily and inexpensively. This was a wonderful way of educating my daughter in the ways of other cultures. Travel has always been my favorite way of learning about the world and it was not hard to get Nilou to enjoy it with me. Before she knew it, she was in a new country or city every few months—before she even started elementary school.

Most people like traveling, but often they just talk about it. They watch TV and movies and see different exciting places and say, "Wow, I wish I was there," or, "One day I'll go there." We just did it. I never waited for the perfect time or to have enough money to travel. We just hopped on the nearest plane, train or even our car and went wherever the wind blew us. I traveled no matter where I lived, and I always took Nilou with me unless she was in school or I was on a business trip.

The Lessons of Travel

Whoever said travel is broadening was very wise. During our years in Europe, Nilou and I saw many cities and countries together. By the time she left elementary school, we had strolled the streets of virtually every major European capitol, from Paris to London, from Amsterdam to Brussels, from Copenhagen to Oslo and so on… During her high school years, we visited, among other places, China, Egypt and Australia. Travel is a gift, and it is the best way to teach your children about different cultures, people and ways of living. By crossing borders, making attempts to speak a foreign tongue, and trying to understand others, your children learn to appreciate people's differences and value them for who they are. No matter how much money you make, no matter what lifestyle you live, I advise you to make traveling a priority. You and your children will learn how other people live, and get some perspective on your own life. You also create the greatest memories traveling with your children.

Together, Nilou and I saw so much: incredible architecture, streets, museums, churches, temples, mosques, gardens, deserts, beaches, oceans, rainforests, towns, villages, different people, different ecosystems and different ways of coping with the daily demands of living. The experience made our lives richer and taught us both things we would never learn by watching television.

I have found one of the greatest challenges in traveling with children is keeping them from being bored or demanding. There has to be balance. If you take your kids on vacations and make them participate in every adult activity, you will lose their interest. On the other hand, if you do everything just to make them happy, then you are traveling on their terms and everyone will miss out on a great deal of culture and beauty. Look for a happy medium: a good mix of cultural activities with other things that children would enjoy. Make some plans for the kids to keep them excited about traveling—stay at hotels with children's activities, look for children's museums, puppet shows and the like. Most of the time, children have no idea of what is going on in a new city. Know how to spark their excitement and interest with simple, sensory things. Don't hustle them out of a place that they like; let them spend more time there. Don't drag them to museums for hour after hour, or they will hate all museums.

If you want your children to love museums, make them fun. Every time Nilou and I went to a museum, we would see everything quickly, talk about a few important points and get out in less than two hours, tops. Then we would go for ice cream or lunch. For Nilou, museums meant fun things; she was one of the few children who liked museums because I didn't make going to them a serious, dull, all-day activity. We saw more than a lot of other families and had fun because we connected the experience to something joyful.

No Trip is Perfect

When it comes to travel, you can never make kids perfectly happy and that's fine. Even if some parts of the trip are boring, you can make others interesting.

I had dreamed of taking a trip to the North Cape of Norway since I was fifteen years old—to see the midnight sun. We went there when I was thirty and Nilou was ten years old. I loved standing on top of the mountains and watching the sun going down, turning orange and red, then to orange and yellow as it rose again. But my beloved daughter thought I was nuts; she couldn't have cared less about the midnight sun. How was I supposed to make the trip interesting for my 10-year-old who just wanted to sit in the hotel room and watch television and eat chips and popcorn?

I compromised. She would go with me and watch the midnight sun one night, and the next night she could stay and watch TV, which was fun for her because we never watched much television at home. During the day, I made our cultural and natural visits more fun by explaining things in a way that would interest her. Children are naturally curious; you just need to stimulate their curiosity.

Travel, travel, travel! Go and see new places, take your children with you, teach them life and don't worry about their complaints. Spend less money on buying clothing, eating out, and everything else you spend money on and save your money for travel. Live life memorably! Create memories of your trips with your children to exotic places. You won't remember trips to the mall, but you will always remember when you climbed the Great Wall of China.

An Exercise

Write down the three new places you want to go with your child in the next three years. If you are not sure, research your idea online and see what kinds of places you could visit—national parks, small towns, big cities, wilderness areas, waterfalls or lakes. Then hold a special family meeting to discuss your idea. Make a plan and map out your travels. Build in something for every member of your family. Talk about things that you want to experience and ask for your children's input. You will soon have your kids addicted to travel.

Different Strokes for Different Folks

During travel, teach your children to understand and appreciate the differences between cultures. This teaches them to appreciate the way they live and everything they have—not to take what they have for granted. Millions of people live with vastly less wealth and fewer possessions than virtually anyone in America. If you have this book in your hand, you live better than ninety percent of the people on Earth. Many people cannot afford food and clean water, much less books and education. Our children don't appreciate this until we show them.

When Nilou and I were in Egypt, we went to some of the smallest villages and islands on the Nile and observed people's lives. We went into their homes and looked at the simple way they lived. We didn't know Arabic and couldn't communicate, but we found locals who could translate and tell us about their simple lives. Many of them lived in simple huts made of hay, with a kitchen in one corner and a few blankets to use both as mattress as well as cover. What struck us most was that despite (or perhaps because of) these humble surroundings, they were content. Children were playing on the dirt road in front of their homes with partially torn clothes and shoes, but they were enjoying themselves. There was a well in the middle of the village and everyone was taking water from it. They were cheerful and full of energy. Everyone lived simply, shared and seemed happy with no need for big screen TVs or video games.

What made those people happy? What were their needs and their wants? By contrast, what were our needs and wants in life? How much did we truly *need*? Nilou and I had long conversations about that, and we still remember what we learned on that trip: happiness doesn't come with material things.

It's your job to help your children think and ask good questions. When you travel, don't spend all your time in the most expensive hotel in town with other tourists. Spend time with locals; speak with them and see how they live, how they work and how they entertain. Partake of their hospitality and honor them with your courtesy. In Egypt, we, too, did the typical touristy activities such as riding a camel and seeing the pyramids, but that was not all we did. In China, of course we saw the Great Wall, the Forbidden City and Tiananmen Square, but we also took a tour with local people. It was not as clean and as comfortable as a tourist-only tour might have been, but we were there to learn about the real life of the Chinese. Mission accomplished.

After you are done with your Eiffel Tower and Notre Dame tour in Paris, spend some time with the little man selling *crepes au chocolat* on a corner in the *Quartier Latin*. Your children need to experience that too. Sometimes, we were invited to people's houses because we had been friendly and chatted with locals. This was the essence, to me, of wonderful traveling. I always loved the chance to see how regular people live in different parts of the world instead of just experiencing the tourist life. Being open and going out of your way to experience local life is the best way in the world to travel.

Demystifying Language

Introducing children to new languages is not difficult if you start early. There is a simple reason for it: every child learns to speak! The skills are the same, so if you can play with different languages before they go to school and even kindergarten, they will not have a hard time mastering more than one. Kids learn to speak the way they are talked to, so if you want to have multi-lingual children, place them in an environment where more than one language is spoken. Let them speak with someone of a different language every day and ask that person to only speak this new language with your child. That person might be you or your parent, a babysitter or a neighbor.

Kids don't have to speak perfect English before they start another language. My daughter speaks five languages fluently, and she started learning English when she was almost twelve. Today she speaks English without any accent and writes it better than many of her schoolmates.

When you already speak a second language at home, you have an advantage. Start speaking that language with your child and refuse to talk if they don't answer you in that language. When Nilou was growing up in Germany, I would not answer her if she spoke with me in German. German was for school and people on the street. Only when she spoke to me in Farsi would I respond. She hated it, but I did whatever it took to help her learn how to read and write in Farsi.

We had our strict rules: in the house we only spoke Farsi, and I took her to her Farsi class every Monday afternoon. She was not very good in class. Writing from right to left, something she was not used to, was not a pleasant experience. What mattered was that she was learning how to read and write in a different language. It was worth the world that she could speak Farsi with my parents when they visited or read signs on the street when we went to Iran to visit. Now that she is older (and thinks she is wiser than me), she appreciates the lessons and blames me for not pushing her more!

There were two reasons I did this. No matter what second language you speak, learning another language helps your brain master future languages more easily. Second, learning any language gives you the ability to communicate with people from other cultures, and that is a requirement for being a superstar. After learning five languages, Nilou sees new languages as something fun. She learns a word or two from every person she meets and she finds similarities between languages. Learning Farsi has also helped keep her more in touch with the country of her origins.

Speaking American

Then we moved to the U.S. and she had to learn English. This was not easy at first. At age twelve, going to school and not understanding almost anything, while sometimes you are being made fun of…that was hard. I found out that children in America make fun of each other more than other places in the world because of language. Speaking English is a big deal because that is the only language most Americans speak.

I remember the day that she came home very sad and said, "Mom, I didn't know what a "thigh" was when our physical education teacher asked us to stretch our thighs. I asked the girl next to me, and she made fun of me. I was so hurt."

I told her, "When you go back to school next day, ask that girl if she knew what the word for thigh was in any other language! Tell her you know it in two other languages!" I talked with her about the fact that she was learning her third language and that girl knew only one. I told her she should be proud of herself for knowing almost every word in two other languages, and that there was no pride in knowing only your native language. I told her that instead of being embarrassed, she should be proud. She started to think that way and see herself as more accomplished than the girl who had mocked her.

Some parents choose the easier way and let their children speak only English, either because they have a provincial view of the world or because they don't want to force their child to work. It is easier not to challenge them and to let them speak their native tongue. I think this is a mistake; it denies children the gift of communicating in a different way, even if the child faces serious challenges in learning the language.

Starting a language is not easy in the American public school system. When Nilou reached the seventh grade, I wanted her to learn two new languages at the same time: French and Spanish. I had serious discussions with the counselors, the principal, and everyone in charge. I was told I could not have my child in two second language classes. She was new in this country, they said. She had just learned to speak English and they could not let her fall behind. German could be considered her second language and would satisfy her academic requirements. That was not why I was fighting.

I wanted my daughter to have more than a good G.P.A. I wanted her to have knowledge for life. After days of arguing, the school officials finally agreed to let her take one additional language; I chose French. I figured she would learn Spanish later because it is so widely spoken in the U.S. So she took French in seventh and eighth grade; later on, after more battles, they let her take Spanish as well. In high school I figured I needed to do more to help her become fluent. She needed to go overseas and speak the languages in their native countries.

Travel as Language Classroom

As a single mom, I couldn't afford $10,000 for some student exchange organization to arrange an exchange trip for Nilou. So I got creative. I started talking to friends in Europe. Because of all the places we have lived, we are blessed with good friends all over the world. I contacted friends with connections in Spain, France and Switzerland until I found a great family for Nilou in Spain. She spent several weeks in Barcelona during one summer, staying with a great family. This experience did not cost me anything—I had flight benefits from United Airlines, so even that part of the trip was free! In return the family sent their daughter to stay with us for several weeks at the end of the summer. After that summer, Nilou became comfortable with Spanish.

A year later, I sent her to Switzerland. She lived in a small French-speaking village where she practiced her French and volunteered for the Red Cross. The Swiss girl from her host family came to stay with us and learned English a few months after that. This turned out to be the most inexpensive way of teaching my daughter, and a fantastic way of meeting new people.

Giving your children the gift of fluency in multiple languages doesn't take money. It takes imagination. All children have the seeds of language genius within them; they can learn more than one language when they are young if you make it fun and interesting. Get creative, start planning right now and have fun raising your multi-lingual superstars.

CHAPTER FIVE:
The Selfless Superstar

The value of a man resides in what he gives and not in what he is capable of receiving.

—*Albert Einstein*

At some point, superstar children have to turn from focusing on themselves to looking at how they can give back to other people, the community, and the world at large. That is what defines a superstar in the end: someone who can make the most of his or her potential and abilities in order to make a positive difference for other people, the environment and the human society. I am proud that is what Nilou is planning to do as she studies international law with a focus on human rights, and your superstars can do the same.

A real superstar has a genuine love for people, even in the face of all their failings. Superstars set aside prejudices and pettiness to focus on the good in everyone and help other people achieve greater prosperity, health and happiness. I don't believe that gifted individuals who achieve great success but don't give back to society deserve to be called superstars. If you have received great gifts from the world, you have a responsibility to give back. As a Hindu proverb says, *"They who give have all things; they who withhold have nothing."*

Contribution means having a loving heart and being mindful of always giving to others while taking for ourselves. We start to plant the seeds of kindheartedness when our children are young. Children see what we do for others, how we talk about others, and what we do to help people. As in all things, they follow our example in seeing what it means to contribute to the world—and they see how good we feel when we give selflessly.

Teaching Selflessness

The sole meaning of life is to serve humanity.
—*Leo Tolstoy*

Teaching Nilou about giving took long conversations, just like in all other areas of our lives. She was very young, maybe three or four years old, when I started. We always talked about ways to help others who needed help, and she knew the things that I did to aid others. She also knew that I had learned about giving from my parents. Their home has always been a center for helping, a place where people can come when in need. They are known for having good hearts and living their lives to give and share with others.

One of Nilou's first experiences with how good it feels to help someone in need goes back to the second grade in Germany. One day, she came home and said, "Mom, I am very sad. It is so unfair that other children are making fun of Saiid." I asked her why the other children were making fun of him. I found out that Saiid was a little Turkish boy from a simple poor family with very little money. He didn't comb his hair and his hands were dry from the cold. He was not very well groomed. After we talked about what we could do for him, we decided to go out and buy him some little gifts.

That day we went to the store and bought a comb, hand cream and a few little things that would help Saiid with his basic hygiene and grooming. We bought a little bag, put everything in it and wrapped it nicely for Nilou to take it to school. But how could we give it to him in a way that would make him feel good, not embarrassed? I called Nilou's teacher, Frau Schierholz, and told her the story. She found our idea cute and she said she would turn it into a nice experience for the class in order to show them that everyone should care for each other. She coordinated the whole thing as a classroom event. Saiid was thrilled to get a gift and Nilou was happy that she could make him happy. From that day on, Saiid was not made fun of anymore. He combed his hair, his hands were clean and Nilou said she saw him a few times putting cream on his little hands. She was thrilled every time she saw it. That was her first lesson in how good it feels to help someone else.

Years later, when she was a junior in high school, we celebrated her birthday at one of the local hospitals by buying cookies for those who didn't have any visitors. Because Nilou's birthday is on Christmas Day, she always got double and triple gifts, so she could afford to miss out on a festive birthday. Giving would be her gift that year.

The morning of her birthday she opened her gifts; then we visited patients in the hospital with cookies that we had bought. We asked the nurses in each station about patients who didn't have any visitors. We went to every one of them, talked to them, wished them happy holidays, and then left the cookies in their rooms. By the end of the day, we were exhausted but very happy. We got such joy from seeing patients' appreciative faces at having visitors on a day when they least expected it, when they assumed everyone was with their families. It was one of the most beautiful birthdays Nilou ever had. We still talk about it. It's a great feeling to be able to give and to see that you can make someone happy. It's even greater to teach it to your children!

A Giving Birthday Tradition

With one success under our belts, Nilou decided to make her twentieth birthday into a fundraising party. She discussed the idea with a club owner in Washington, D.C. and convinced him to let her throw her party there. The cover charge for that night, plus everyone's birthday gift to her (she asked people to give money as a donation), was donated for relief for the massive earthquake that hit the ancient Iranian city of Bam. Nilou enjoyed her birthday and raised more than $1,600 for a great cause. The money went to Iran to my high school principal from more than twenty years ago, who was helping to build a school in Bam at that time.

Nilou advertised her party all over Georgetown University. The club even printed out special invitation cards for her for free! Everyone had fun, and the money went to a place that needed it. This is what I call purposeful living. We need to help our children become more creative, make purposeful decisions, and give back to the community and the world. I get such joy out of seeing that my daughter has a purpose in her life beyond her own pleasure.

Today, helping others and contributing to the community have become part of Nilou's spirit, something she integrates into her life all the time. She has worked as a volunteer at a Skills Center in San Francisco teaching reading, writing and computer skills to homeless adults. She has helped non-profit organizations do research they need to know how best to help the homeless with housing, food and education. She has volunteered on international projects in Argentina and the Middle East. She is the president of the Human Rights group and Vice President of Amnesty International at Georgetown Law School. Her goal is admirable: to do everything in her power to protect the unheard, the poor, the uneducated and underprivileged.

An Adventure with Grandma

Millions of young people around the world do wonderful things for others every day, and we never hear about them. This is a story I was told recently, and I want to share it with you:

> *I remember my first Christmas adventure with Grandma. I was just a kid. I remember tearing across town on my bike to visit her on the day my big sister dropped the bomb: "There is no Santa Claus," she jeered. "Even dummies know that!"*
>
> *My Grandma was not the gushy kind. I fled to her that day because I knew she would be straight with me. I knew Grandma always told the truth, and it always went down a lot easier when swallowed with one of her world-famous cinnamon buns. I knew they were world-famous, because Grandma said so. It had to be true.*
>
> *Grandma was home, and the buns were still warm. Between bites, I told her everything. She was ready for me. "No Santa Claus!" she snorted. "Ridiculous! That rumor has been going around for years, and it makes me plain mad. Now, put on your coat, and let's go."*
>
> *"Go where, Grandma?" I asked. "Where" turned out to be Kerby's General Store, the one store in town that had a little bit of everything. As we walked through its doors, Grandma handed me ten dollars. That was a bundle in those days. "Take this money," she said, "and buy something for someone who needs it. I'll wait for you in the car." Then she turned and walked out.*

CHAPTER 5 - THE SELFLESS SUPERSTAR

I was only eight years old. I'd often gone shopping with my mother, but never had I shopped for anything all by myself. The store seemed big and crowded, full of people scrambling to finish their Christmas shopping. For a few moments I just stood there confused, clutching that ten-dollar bill, wondering what to buy and who on earth to buy it for.

I thought of everybody I knew: my family, my friends, my neighbors, the kids at school, and the people at my church. I was just about thought out when I suddenly thought of Bobby Decker. He was a kid with bad breath and messy hair, and he sat right behind me in Mrs. Pollock's grade-two class.

Bobby Decker didn't have a coat. I knew that because he never went out for recess during winter. His mother always wrote a note, telling the teacher that he had a cough, but we knew that Bobby Decker didn't have a coat. I fingered the ten-dollar bill with growing excitement. I would buy Bobby Decker a coat!

I settled on a red corduroy coat with a hood. It looked warm. "Is this a Christmas present for someone?" the lady behind the counter asked kindly as I laid my ten dollars down. "Yes," I replied shyly. "It's....for Bobby." The nice lady smiled at me. She put the coat in a bag and wished me a Merry Christmas.

That evening, Grandma helped me wrap the coat in Christmas paper and ribbons (a little tag fell out of the coat, and Grandma tucked it in her Bible) and wrote, "To Bobby, From Santa Claus" on it—Grandma said that Santa always insisted on secrecy. Then she drove me over to Bobby Decker's house, explaining as we went that I was now and forever officially one of Santa's helpers.

Grandma parked down the street from Bobby's house, and she and I crept noiselessly and hid in the bushes by his front walk. Then Grandma gave me a nudge. "All right, Santa Claus," she whispered, "get going."

I took a deep breath, dashed for his front door, threw the present down on his step, pounded his doorbell and flew back to the safety of the bushes and Grandma. Together we waited breathlessly in the darkness for the front door to open. Finally it did, and there stood Bobby.

Fifty years haven't dimmed the thrill of those moments spent shivering beside my Grandma in Bobby Decker's bushes. That night, I realized that those awful rumors about Santa Claus were just what Grandma said they were: ridiculous.

Santa was alive and well, and we were on his team. I still have the Bible, with the coat's price tag tucked inside: $19.95.

Exercise

Think about one way in which you can take action in your community today, or one way you can do something nice for someone in need. It doesn't matter whether the thing you do is big or small. The goal is to bring light into someone's life. Plan on doing something you have never done before, something new to your children. Think about it, write it down, discuss it with your children, make a plan and take action.

CHAPTER 5 - THE SELFLESS SUPERSTAR

_____
_____
_____
_____
_____
_____
_____
_____
_____
_____
_____
_____
_____
_____
_____
_____

Be aware, however, that even the most kindhearted child needs encouragement to volunteer. Children are fundamentally selfish. They like to think about their own needs from the time they are born. Opening their eyes to the wonders of giving to others elevates them above this selfish nature. When they are young, even before they start school, is the perfect time to teach them do things that help them grow into better adults. What if you encourage them to give half of the balloons and gifts that they received for their birthday to a poor child? What if you take them to a shelter or foster home and help them experience the great feeling of giving to others and making other children happy? Allow your children to experience this feeling at early age.

When they are older, encourage them to volunteer or do charity work and support them in their efforts. Go with them to a local church, synagogue, mosque, temple, hospital, or homeless shelter and talk with someone in charge about giving some time each week. Help them connect with a group that cleans up local beaches or delivers books to local libraries. There are a hundred ways they can give and enjoy doing it. Help them develop the mindset that they should always be thinking, "What else can I do?" and "How else can I give and make a difference in other people's lives"?

It's great if they get college credit, but that should be the least of their concerns. Giving is its own reward. Your job is helping your kids understand the *meaning* of giving. You make a difference in your world and the world your children will inherit by teaching them the beauty and the power of giving. Teach your children to view the rest of the world just as important as their immediate surroundings.

Love for the World

> *It is not the magnitude of our actions but the amount of love that is put into them that matters.*
> —*Mother Teresa*

The Beatles said, "Love is all you need." Is that really true? Let's think for a moment. What would the world be like if we all loved each other? How would it be if we stopped the feelings of hatred by not teaching our children to hate anyone? Some people say that is not realistic, that hate is part of being human and a world without it is impossible to imagine. I disagree. I think hate is a habit that we teach our children, and we can teach them love for everyone just as easily.

What if you let go of every argument about politics, religion, and race and started teaching your child to love everyone, just because it feels better? How does feeling love and being loved make you feel? Warm, safe, hopeful and worthy perhaps? If everyone felt that way, the world would change. Wouldn't it? We would have no wars, because people who cherish each other don't kill. It would end hunger and poverty, because we would all gladly share something of what we have with our brothers and sisters. Love would not end disease, but it would make us put all our efforts into curing it. Love would make the world a better place to live; it would make it a paradise. So why not teach our children to love everyone, no matter who they are, what they believe or how they live? Why not give them that advantage?

Teach Acceptance

My greatest reward as a parent is when I see Nilou shows unconditional love to the world. People who are filled with genuine love, love that is not self-serving but selflessly giving, shine with a visible light.

What if your children were not allowed to hate anyone? What if the focus of their education, along with reading and writing, was on making the world a better place for everyone and teaching love from early on in life? We could parent in such a way that our children were not allowed to make fun of others but start understanding them instead. Acceptance should be our greatest lesson—that just because someone worships a different god, has a different skin color, has different political beliefs, or was born in a third world country doesn't mean he or she is any less important or worthwhile than they are. Just because someone is making less money or has a different job, we don't categorize them as lower-quality human beings.

In bringing about this grand global transformation, we would have to lead by example. We, as parents would have to stop gossiping and criticizing our in-laws, ex-spouses, co-workers and people with whom we disagree. We would have to shed our shallow prejudices and wish everyone peace, health and love. Could you do this? Is it worth it, if you could give your children the advantage of universal love as they grow?

Don't underestimate your children. They are smart and they listen to everything you say. Don't think they cannot hear you in the other room or when they play with their friends. When you badmouth someone, they hear. They mimic. They learn by your actions that it is OK to talk about people hatefully, critically and angrily. A few shortsighted words from you can shape their ideas about others for years.

Nilou and I live our lives with love for all, and it really works. We remind ourselves everyday to keep this habit. It has made our lives joyful. We have always discussed what we can learn from the people in our lives and practiced seeing at least one good thing in every person. We didn't necessarily stay close to everyone we met; I would not suggest that to anybody. It's not realistic. You don't have to become everyone's best friend. What we learned is to not hate someone just because they were cruel to us or because we didn't agree with some aspect of their lives. My theory is that people do their best at any given time, even if it might not be the best for us. That approach is wonderful for forgiveness and understanding. Raise forgiving, understanding children and they will feel good every day of their lives.

The End of Envy

If you judge people, you have no time to love them.
— Mother Teresa

Work with your kids to kill the roots of jealousy and unhealthy competition. Competition is fine, but envy for someone else's success is poisonous. Today, when Nilou hears about someone excelling in something, instead of being jealous, she tries to get to know that person. When she was a child, I taught her that successful people can teach everyone something, so you should learn from them, not envy them. I started this training when she was very young, and we had some battles over enforcement when she was in high school. But today I see the great result.

Nilou has the habit of making friends with the most successful people around her. Every time she gets to know that person more, she feels better about herself. Becoming friends with smart, talented, competitive people—people who might otherwise intimidate her—has helped her realize that they are human like everyone else. She now knows that we are all geniuses in something. We all have strengths that can be shared with others and we all have weaknesses that friends can help us overcome. Nilou learned to be thankful for her strengths while appreciating those of others. Now she is blessed with a circle of great, loving friends who she teaches and from whom she learns every day.

Exercise

Write down the names of three of the most loving people you know, those you always like to be around. Think about the things they do, the way they talk and interact with others. What can you learn from them? What do they have in common? What can you take from them and bring into your life? Write that one thing down and talk about it with your children. Make it like a family project and work on it.

_____
_____
_____
_____
_____

CHAPTER 5 - THE SELFLESS SUPERSTAR

Love Makes a Difference

One of the daily conversations Nilou and I had was about handling difficult situations and loving people in spite of their difficulties. I told her that, as exhausted as I was with my multiple moves between different countries and continents, and as hurt or disappointed as I was in my relationships, my mantra was, "This, too, shall pass." There's no point in letting ourselves be dragged down by bad memories; they do us no good. Instead, I taught her to look at the bright side and always wish everyone the best.

I didn't hate Nilou's father for abandoning us. I saw it as his loss and our gain, and I still see it that way. His betrayal of us was a sign of his weakness, not some unworthiness in me. Instead, I am thankful that I had the opportunity to grow and make a life on my own, because I am a better, stronger person now than if I had depended on him. I remember at one point Nilou felt vengeful towards him and started having some negative thoughts. I reminded her that she was born because he and I loved each other. She was a product of love even if it didn't last. She forgave him and lives her life with boundless love and positive energy.

This should be the ultimate goal for your superstar child: to make the world to a better place because they live in it. What more important goal is there? We are all part of the same family, and when we love each other as family, we can do astonishing things. Teach your children to let go of bad things and allow them to experience freedom from negativity and the greatness of love.

Exercise

Write down five things you will (or will not) do in order to teach your child to become a loving person. It might be helping your child come up with ideas for giving back in the community, or stopping hateful talk about your ex-spouse or in-laws. How can you focus your lives on love, rather than intolerance or resentment? What can you start immediately that will help your child become a loving superstar? Read and repeat it every day. Live it with your children. Teach them to love and you will teach them to live well.

_____
_____
_____
_____
_____
_____
_____
_____
_____
_____
_____
_____
_____

CHAPTER SIX:
The Superstar Family

The family is the country of the heart. There is an angel in the family who, by the mysterious influence of grace, of sweetness, and of love, renders the fulfillment of duties less wearisome, sorrows less bitter. The only pure joys unmixed with sadness given to man to taste upon earth are, thanks to this angel, the joys of the family.

—**Giuseppe Mazzini, Italian nationalist leader**

No superstar succeeds alone. No matter how gifted or driven your child is, he or she needs your assistance to make it to the top. As you walk the road of growth and development with your superstar, you are going to find yourselves pulled in two directions as the years pass and your child becomes an adolescent. One direction will be that of independence and separation as your child moves into activities that take up much of his or her time, makes new friends that detract from family involvement, and simply wants to explore the wider world. The other direction will be your desire to keep your child close to the family, not to lose the contact and closeness that you have cherished over the years. I will tell you that in my experience, it is vital to strike a balance between the two, but you should err on the side of keeping your superstar within the loving arms of the family.

Yes, I have talked about how important it is that your child becomes independent and develops that "self starter" quality that is so crucial to success. And you certainly don't want to retard your child's development with regard to friends or relationships. But in this culture, where so many parents and children are estranged as the years pass, I cannot overemphasize the importance of keeping close family ties when your child is ten years old or forty years old. Quite simply, children who grow up feeling like they always have a place in the family where they are loved and listened to (even if they choose not to take advantage of it all the time) are more confident, happier, and have stronger self-esteem. There will never be a substitute for family and home. As poet Robert Frost wrote, *"Home is the place that when you go there, they have to take you in."*

Family Meetings

Since Nilou was small, we have had family meetings, even though, with just the two of us, our meetings were less like a Board of Directors and more like a player and her coach. I am a big believer in family meetings that are held regularly. These are times you can use to build confidence and develop your communication with your children. When you have an established family meeting time where the boundaries are clear and everyone feels safe, it is a wonderful way to learn about what you need to know as a parent:

- What your children have been doing
- What your children's friends are doing
- What their wishes are
- Their goals
- Possible sources of stress outside the home
- How your spouse is dealing with family issues
- Problems and potential crises
- Fun things the family could do together
- How each person can support the others in achieving goals for the coming week, month or year

Family meetings are open forums where everyone is encouraged to communicate openly and share their feelings without fear of being laughed at or disciplined. In a family you and your children are NOT equals (more about this later), but in the meeting environment, where everyone gets his or her time on the floor, you are as close to equals as possible. This demonstrates to children that they are listened to and encourages them to listen to and respect their parents and siblings. Open communication was very important in my relationship with Nilou, and continues to be the foundation of our family. Meetings make that kind of communication a positive family habit.

In our family, family meetings were on Friday nights. We usually ordered food, rented a movie we knew we would both like, and watched it at the end of our meeting. This became our "stay home and spend time with family" night. We stayed home and talked about what happened during the week. Our family meeting time was Friday night because Nilou didn't have school the next day, so we could enjoy our time without worries about homework and being sleepy the next morning. This also let me keep her home on Friday nights when she was in high school, which was a common night for big parties, lots of alcohol, and dangerous drivers on the roads.

During the week we always sat at the kitchen table for dinner, and we would also talk then. Eating in front of the TV and in the family room was forbidden on most nights because I believed (and still believe) that it would create distance between us rather than closeness. I still do not allow it when she is home from school. I believe a family should sit around the dinner table, eat together, talk and simply share the joy of being in the same space and time. For our meeting night we were allowed to break the rule. This was the only time we made an exception.

How to Hold a Family Meeting

I built my meetings with Nilou around dinner, with the promise of a movie at the end, to make them more fun for both of us. Food brought us to the table for a reason other than talking, which was always helpful. And the promise of a movie or some other form of entertainment gave us something to look forward to doing as a family, so we didn't just scatter when the meeting was over. We spent the entire Friday evening together. At the end of the night we spoke about the movie, which part of it we liked most and what we learned.

Family meeting time is about getting together, talking about what we did, what we want to do and how we can help each other out, planning together and enjoying the end of the day together. You bring the family together and talk about what went on during the last week, special times at school or at work, what was good, what was bad, and what could be better. Did someone hurt another person's feelings? This is the time to talk it out. Did a child do something nice for someone else and felt great about it? Now is the time to share that feeling. Plan summer trips, winter vacations, additions to the house, what new friends are doing and so on. Things that you share at your family meetings will be things you remember for life.

I know a family with two young children who started the meeting habit when their kids were very young. They would go out to dinner every Thursday night and have their meeting. On that night alone, the children were allowed to sleep in their parents' room, read special books, and watch special family movies. For this family, Thursday nights have become a treat, something to look forward to. The outside world is shut off and only the family matters in this oasis of time. No phones, no e-mail, no computers. Now this wise mother and father are building on their family Thursdays as their children grow older, making it more of a family meeting night with planning, constructive criticism, feedback, and open communication.

Some families mix things up a bit: they add a board game or card game to the festivities, so that family night ends with a game. Game or no game, pick a night for your family meetings and work in activities that are fun and nurturing for everyone, so you can make it a night everyone looks forward to. Children want to be heard and want to have a voice in how the family is run. When you make them feel heard and give them your full attention, you have the raw material of some incredible memories.

"We play games at the table and talk about things during the day," says Andy, whom we met earlier. "Heidi's dad eats with us and we make it a family time. We make it a point to sit down every night for dinner and talk together. We talk about business, us, school, life or we play a game. Friday is our night for family meetings, and we use it to talk about everything and anything the family decides and we do something special all together. We watch a video at home, play cards or a board game, whatever the family decides. Each child has a 'dream board' to show their future dreams, and we teach them how to use it. It helps us raise them to who THEY want to become."

What is Quality Time?

Is taking a child to the movies quality time? How about watching their soccer game? How do we define quality time? Quality time is important because a family meeting cannot be the only occasion when you give attention to your children. A healthy family—and a healthy, developing superstar—must include ample quality time because the family relationship is more important than shopping, TV, entertainment, pop culture, friends or anything else.

I define quality time as the time when parent and child are together "actively," each giving something to the other, not just occupying the same space. During quality time, you and your child might discuss something, teach and learn, communicate, travel, play a game, cook a meal or do anything where everyone is involved. Quality time means giving your attention to your child and demanding that your child's attention be given to you, so you are both present in the moment.

Unfortunately, some parents mistake "quantity time" for quality time. I think this is an effort to assuage their own guilt at not stopping their own multitasking lives for a short while and making the time to "be" with their children. Let me be clear: quality time is not going to the mall and shopping, something that many moms do every weekend to get closer to their girls. It is not Dads going to electronics stores with the boys to buy videogames. Quality time is not something you can buy. Quality time is something you *create*. It involves communication and sharing and learning. Some examples of quality time:

- Sitting with your daughter or son and talking about things that give them joy in school and after school, or things that hurt their feelings
- Having dinner around the table every night with the family and taking your time for being together at dinner

- Allowing everyone to speak about the happenings during the day at the dinner table
- Going on an outing to a zoo or a museum, or going on a picnic
- Going to lunch or dinner and just talking without worrying about schedules
- Preparing a meal together and learning from each other about cooking and what foods you both like or dislike
- Gardening together
- Working on a project together, such as planning a party or building something

Make the Time, Even if It is Short

I can hear the objections already, the busy parents lamenting, "I don't have time to go to lunch with my oldest," or "I work late every night." Well, I am sorry, but it's time to decide what your priorities are. It doesn't require a major sacrifice to have quality time with your kids. You can have it while you are cooking dinner, with your children sitting at the kitchen table doing their homework, with both of you talking about your days. As long as you can speak and share, you can teach your children much about communication, trust and courtesy—and show them they are the most important parts of your life.

When Nilou was twelve years old, I borrowed two books about manners from the local library. We had the greatest time with those books. We would pick a chapter each day and read and analyze it together. We learned things like the European manners I had taught her when she was growing up in Germany were not the same as American table manners. We learned and discussed phone manners in different settings. We learned some of the more traditional and interesting manners and we still remember those discussions. We learned fascinating things together and had great fun at the same time.

You can always have quality time with your children no matter what you do and how busy your life is. Even if you only have one hour per day to give to your child, as long as it is a meaningful hour where you shut everything else down and listen to your child, share yourself and make the time count, you've got your quality time. Remember, it is called "quality time," not "quantity time."

Quality time is not taking your children from one class to another while you talk on your cell phone and they watch DVDs in the car. Time and attention are some of the most precious gifts you can give your child, and an essential part of any family. Play with your children, listen to them, encourage them to develop their personalities, correct inappropriate behavior while having fun, and teach life lessons.

Love and Appreciation

And so we come to love, the single most essential ingredient for a flourishing family and a superstar child. Love is the soil in which the family grows, and the health of that family depends on the quality of that soil. If it is rich, deep, fragrant and filled with the nutrients of care, discipline, guidance, time, fun and respect, then the family and children will grow tall and strong and blossom into greatness. If it is hard, sparse and laden with little more than the weeds of neglect, permissiveness and resentment, then the family will suffer and children will not grow into who they can be. In what kind of soil is your family planted?

The single most important thing you can give to your children is unconditional and unlimited love. Love them for who they are. Love them for nothing more than being your children. Show them that your unconditional love is timeless, limitless and appears in endless ways in their lives. Love forms the firm foundation for children to walk on as they grow into young adults and venture into the world. No matter what happens to them or how anxious they become as they confront obstacles, they always have the touchstone of your love to let them know someone cares and always rejoices in what they achieve. Children who are deeply loved are free to try and fail, knowing that what they do doesn't matter; you will always love them no matter what.

Children perceive love in different ways. Some need it through words. Others need it expressed physically—hugs, kisses, tickles, and such. Express your love for your child in every way you can imagine, because it all makes a difference. Give them little gifts once in a while and do it with excitement and passion. It is not the material gift that matters; it is about bringing excitement and beautiful moments to daily living.

Money Can't Buy Me Love

No material possession, no matter how wonderful, can ever make up for parental neglect. The biggest flat panel TV, the coolest video game or the greatest pair of shoes will not make your children feel as loved as an hour of your time spent talking with them, asking them about school and hugging them at the end of the hour.

Unfortunately, in our culture it is common for parents to buy their children expensive toys to make up for mistakes and time that they don't spend with them. Do not ever do this. It solves nothing, and in a way, it tells your child that your love is so cheap it can be substituted for by a computer game. Your love for your child is worth far more! Instead, buy small, special things once in a while that show thought and care. When you buy gifts or small surprises, you teach your children to be happy with little wonders. Also, your own excitement and happiness with the gift will rub off on them. Make every little thing a great surprise rather than an expectation. Even an ice cream or a candy can be a nice gift if you present it with excitement and passion. By practicing this with your children when they are young, you will prevent them from developing a sense of entitlement and teach them to appreciate genuine gestures of love and not be fooled by flashy, empty gestures.

You can show your love in the home you create for your kids. Create a warm, pleasant environment in your house, with flowers and beauty. Encourage your kids to participate in creating the look and feel of a room in your home. Give each child a private space to store their things, or if you have the luxury, give them each a private nook or room of their own that can be their personal space.

It is vital to constantly remind your children of your love in words. It is the rare child who doesn't enjoy hearing loving words, praise and appreciation. Give them what they need—praise them for being who they are. Compliment them on their strongest attributes as well as their weaker attributes. Your compliments will help them be more self-confident. Play with them, read to them and remind them that they can achieve anything and become anyone they want to become. You are the source of your child's power and confidence.

Little Things Mean a Lot

Love also means encouraging your children to remember your love even when it's not expressed on the spot. In other parts of this book, we talk about not doing everything possible for your children in order to teach them independence. When you follow this rule and don't always do nice things for your children, they will appreciate the special treats and gestures even more. This is called "managing expectations." It is also called "not spoiling your children." Small gestures have much more impact when they don't appear all the time. When you teach your children to not expect and not to demand, you are also teaching them to be grateful and thankful.

I didn't have the luxury of being there all the time for my daughter, but I was there for Nilou anytime that she needed me. She never missed me when I was needed. She felt my love, heard it and saw it. I hugged, kissed and praised her. I gave her great compliments. I told her how much I loved her every single day. Even when she was in high school, when the risk of parental embarrassment is critically high, a hug and kiss were part of our daily plan. She knew Mom needed a hug when we both got home. If she was in trouble in school, if she was in pain because of things that were going on in her young heart, she knew she could always talk to me. She felt the love that was there for her and she trusted our relationship.

Some days I would buy flowers, put them on the table and I would tell her that the flowers were for her and because I loved her, and I wanted her to know that. Small gifts that I knew would make her happy were always part of our life, but they were always surprises—never a given. I never gave her things exactly when she wanted them. I was not what I call a "vending machine parent"—just push the button and whatever is needed falls. I waited for an occasion. I always wrapped things nicely, and took the time. It was not about the money I spent, but rather about the time and thoughts I spent.

Now I see the results. On my birthday, holidays or Mother's Day, I get the most beautiful cards with beautiful handwritten notes. Nilou is just practicing what I taught her when she was in college, when she could count on receiving motivational and loving cards from me every few weeks. The care package from home, that was OK, but it was something every student got. The personal, meaningful cards were what were special to her.

Be generous in giving love! Say it and show it in every possible way. Don't assume that your children will perceive love the way you do. If you are a touchy, feely person, it doesn't mean they are exactly like you. They might recoil from too much hugging and prefer honest, simple words of love. They might like surprises (I think all children do). They might like expressions of love that are not even on your mind. Speak with them about it. Learn the way they perceive your love. Ask them about things that make them happy and feel loved. Ask about the moments that they felt most loved. Once you learn how they want to be loved, remind them of your love every single day. Tell them what you love most about them and make it specific. Put it on your to-do list: "Love my child."

Exercise

Write down five different ways you think you expressed your love to your child in the last week. Then ask your child about how many times they remember you letting them know that you love them. Did they remember all the times you did? Are you making an impression on your little one?

Tell your children you are reading this book and saw this exercise there. Ask them what they think. Ask if they perceived love from you. What thing you did gave them the most feeling of being loved? Which one did they like most?

If you have more than one child, you will notice how different children perceive love differently.

CHAPTER 6 - THE SUPERSTAR FAMILY

After this exercise, please e-mail me at terri@RaisingASuperstar.com and let me know how it turned out. What were the five ways that you thought you were giving, showing and sharing love, and what made the strongest impression on your kids?

In the end, family is all about love shown in every way, but most of all by your actions. The things you do that show love and respect for other family members, the small kindnesses you show your children and your spouse, how high a priority you give to making time for your children over your job and other concerns, the time you spend each day just asking a few questions—these all speak volumes more loudly than any words of love or approval.

Act with love every day, speak the important words to remind your kids that you adore and cherish them, hug them, hold them and surprise them with gestures and little gifts from time to time to create delight in their lives. That is the love of a family and it will travel with them all their lives.

CHAPTER SEVEN:
The Well-Rounded Superstar

Finding the perfect balance is getting harder and harder. We need to teach our children to be cautious without imparting fear, to learn right from wrong without being judgmental, to be assertive but not pushy, to stick to routines without sacrificing spontaneity, and to be determined but not stubborn.
—*Fred G. Gosman*
"How to Be a Happy Parent...In Spite of Your Children"

We are close to the end of our journey together, and I am deeply grateful for the time you have given me so far. I trust it has been worth it as you have seen the lessons that I learned in my own challenging journey raising a driven, astonishing child. And I hope some of my meager wisdom has encouraged you to look at your own children in a new way, to see them as young people with limitless potential and possibility for the future.

Here, in the last chapter, I wrap things up by asking a simple but vital question: in a world where so many people go astray, how do you keep your superstar mentally and emotionally healthy, focused on the good things in life, and headed in a direction that promises greater love, joy and purpose in the years to come?

Interest in Many Things

I don't believe in specialization for children. Even if they express a desire to get into a career that is very demanding, such as medicine or law, they can lead balanced, stress-free lives by cultivating interests in diverse areas. Keeping your children busy and helping them pursue their curiosity with different hobbies, avocations and areas of study will keep them out of trouble and create greater opportunities for them later in life.

Start early, maybe as soon as age three or four. It takes more time and energy to steer kids toward varied pursuits if you wait until they are in their teens. By then, they are in their "lazy" teenage mode where all they want to do is play electronic games, watch television, hang out with their friends and defy whatever it is you want them to do. Then you've created more work for yourself. When it comes to hobbies, the younger the better. The best thing about beginning early immersion in many activities is that it forces your kids to get out in the world and meet people. They become less likely to be isolated when they meet like-minded kids who share their passions.

I started Nilou's activities when she was four years old. As I have discussed earlier, she started with ballet and music lessons; she went from there to painting and on and on. She stopped some activities and started others in elementary school. She knew she was not allowed to be lazy around our house. There was no TV in the evening; she had to do something productive with her mind. No negotiation. So when Nilou was home and during weekends, we would go to things like air shows, Broadway shows, parades, soccer games, tennis matches, dance parties, gatherings with family friends and everything possible. So my girl was exposed to many different ways of living, pursuits and types of people. No narrow existence for my daughter!

In middle school and high school, Nilou took activity to an extreme I couldn't believe. It was as if sitting still were illegal. She became involved with almost every club and participated in practically every after school activity that was offered. I would hear from neighbors that she was in the local newspaper. She started to become a public figure when she was in high school and she did it on her own. At that point, she didn't need my encouragement anymore. She knew she could not go out and party with other kids every other night, watch TV at home or be on the Internet. The only way she could keep busy and enhance her social life was by getting involved in healthy activities and by reading.

Among other groups, she joined the Youth Court Team and Model Congress—signs of what would become her future college course of study and her eventual career. These activities effectively formed her future as a lawyer, debater and speaker who has received several speaking awards.

Guide Them… or Just Enroll Them

When you get your children active in many different areas, you help them choose their future with greater confidence. When they get at least a taste of everything around them, they will not end up with a career they simply fall into. Instead, they will choose their life's work because they know something of it and can go into it with passion.

If your child is not active in many things, start with one. Don't wait for your child to tell you what they want to be part of; many times, they will not. Instead, take the initiative and enroll them in a sports program or a cultural course. Get them involved and interested in just one activity, then start the next thing. Get them into the flow of meeting new people and trying new things, even if they are not particularly good at some of them. Set aside brainstorming time, spend time with their friends, and take them to different places. Send them to leadership and discovery camps. You might have to travel or send them to a different city to get them active. Do it if you can. It's worth it. You might be taking your child outside his or her comfort zone, and that's OK. In fact, I encourage that.

At the same time, do not exhaust your children to make yourself feel like a good parent. I am not suggesting that you become one of those parents who drag their children to activities every moment of the day until the children hate everything they do. Every second of your child's life doesn't need to be occupied; children need time to relax, invent, imagine and enjoy simple things.

When you expand your children's interests and expand their minds, you start them in a pattern to use their energy in healthy ways. I guarantee you that if they are engaged in this sport and that cultural activity and involved in this and that club on campus, they will not have the time to get into trouble and hang out with the wrong crowd. They will be too proud of their own industry and achievements to want to spend time with young people who are negative role models.

If you want to raise a superstar—a happy, healthy, well-rounded and balanced person—start to broaden their interests today. If one thing doesn't work, try another. Ignore the "I don't want to, Mom," whining. Kids have no idea what they are missing when they refuse to try an activity, so explain to them that they have to try for a certain length of time, and if they don't like it, they can quit after their trial period. But no one gets away without trying.

Having broad interests means that when one activity is not going well others are there to boost their spirits. So do yourself and your children a favor and get them involved in activities. You can find many that are cheap or even free through your city or school, including things like martial arts, dance, gymnastics, art classes, music, gardening, science clubs, language clubs and much more.

Exercise

Write down three different activities in which you can start your child immediately. Do your research and choose three that suit your child best, and over the next six weeks, start your child in all three activities. They could be sports, arts, school clubs or anything you can imagine. Ask your child for a list of after-school activities. Sit down with your child and choose the best activity together. Call other parents with active children and suggest a carpool if your time is limited. Get creative and start the excitement!

Teach Them to Adapt

Things in life don't always go as planned. Plans fall apart, people let us down, or divorce and disease sometimes step in the way of what we had in mind for ourselves. This can be especially hard for children to deal with, because they have grown up with their parents making all the hard times go away. But superstars learn to adapt to what life throws their way, so they can rise above it and still achieve their goals. But adaptability is not in the DNA; it must be taught.

When we raise our children to be adaptable, we teach them how to cope with changes and challenges in life, how to live with different people, and how to get past disappointments and realize that a single failure is not the end and can, in fact, be a new beginning.

Nilou and I were fortunate enough to be able to move to different continents, countries, cities and towns. I call it lucky; some people call it disaster when they have to move their children from one street to another in the same neighborhood! They see change as the enemy, damaging their children's fragile minds. Well, let me tell you, children's minds are not so fragile. They are pretty resilient, as long as you, their parents, are resilient. If they see you handling change with aplomb, they will handle it the same way.

My experience is that change during childhood makes children stronger and helps them become adults who live easily in any new environment. It all depends on how you make change look to their innocent eyes. Remember, change by itself is neither negative nor positive; it takes on the meaning that you give to it. Children have questions about the unknown, they have emotional issues, and they have fear of the unknown and fear of loss. When things change, they worry they will lose their friends and everything else they are familiar with; they don't know anything about the new situation. It's up to you to paint the new situation for them. Which colors will you pick? Which colors have you picked in the past for your children to go through change? How did you color your move, job loss, your divorce or separation, or whatever major change occurred? You can and should shape your child's perspective positively and help them adapt.

Introduce Change

I always assured Nilou that she could keep her friendships with good people no matter how far we moved. I taught her about the value of staying connected when we changed cities or continents. I worked with her to get her excited about making new connections with the new and wonderful people that we would meet, and I talked with her about how much more we can learn and love. Change became an exciting thing in our lives together. If you can train yourself to see change this way and teach your children the same, you will have taught them to enter any new environment and be successful.

Of course, you don't have to relocate to teach your child to be adaptable. There are many ways that you can put your child in new environments to help them learn to adapt and adjust. Don't send them with the same children from the same school to the same camp every year. Get them into a new environment (over their inevitable protests) so they can make new friends and mingle with others. You will create an opportunity for them to be with others, live with others, enjoy others, make friends, and become a loving, interested, interesting person.

If your children have lived a quiet, unchanging life up to now, I suggest you start planning challenging new activities with them. This could be an exotic trip where they have to mingle with other children, an exchange with someone in another country, a camp where they would not see any of their friends—anything that would put them in a new situation where they must handle everything on their own and learn about life. It will be a hard sell. We all want to take the path of least resistance, especially when we are young. New experiences are scary. Your child will not be very happy with change. It is up to you to make it an exciting experience and tell them about all the good things that they are going to learn and discover.

Children who learn to live with different people, deal with many different situations, and maintain their poise no matter what life throws their way become rich adults. They know how to meet new people in any situation and they relish meeting new friends and experiencing new situations. If you know you can take your 18-year-old, give him/her a passport, some money and nothing else, and drop them off in the middle of a major city somewhere in the world knowing they can take care of themselves, you are raising a superstar.

Life: A Balancing Act

Now, we have many pieces of this puzzle called your child. We have adaptability, athletics, learning, family time, leadership, independence and so much more. How do we make all the pieces fit? The truth is they will never fit together in the same way for the same two children. But like the great masters, balancing all the many elements is the way to create great art, and the way to create a life that is a masterpiece. You need to encourage balance in every aspect of your child's life.

By encouraging our children to do different things and getting them interested in different areas of life, we teach them

CHAPTER 7 - THE WELL-ROUNDED SUPERSTAR

balance. Raising a superstar doesn't mean having a child who is successful only in their schoolwork and career, or one who is happy in their own life but cares nothing for the needs of others in the community or the world, or one who is an athletic champion with no time for a personal life. A true superstar balances everything important in life: work, money, family, friends, creativity, health, hobbies and giving back to the community and the world.

Superstar kids who can manage this balancing act turn out to be successful, happy, healthy, loving, caring, confident, knowledgeable, well-rounded leaders. They make a difference in the world and make it a better place. They fill you with pride, because you can say with confidence that if you had to raise them all over again, you would not change a thing. That is not to say you didn't make mistakes; every parent does. But when the outcome is this wonderful, you have done something right. A superstar child frees you from worry, because you know they will always come out on top. The world is their oyster, and in each part of it—personal, professional and charitable—you will find pearls.

Exercise

A superstar's balanced life is like a wheel and each wedge of the wheel an aspect of that life. Here, label each section of this wheel with the various aspects of your child's life—Family, School, Friends, Physical, Emotional and Extracurricular. Then assign a percentage to each based on how great you feel they are in that area of life. If the center of the circle represents

0% and the outside of the circle represents 100% of where you want your child to be in this area of life, where do you think your child is currently in each area? Where would you score them in their physical and athletic life? Where are they in academics, do they give their best to their school? How about being surrounded by excellent friends who influence them to become better people while they are having fun? How do they value family? How balanced is your child's life? Are some activities getting an eighty or ninety score while others get only five or ten? Maybe it's time to talk about those areas that need more attention so you can help your child have a life that is truly balanced in every area.

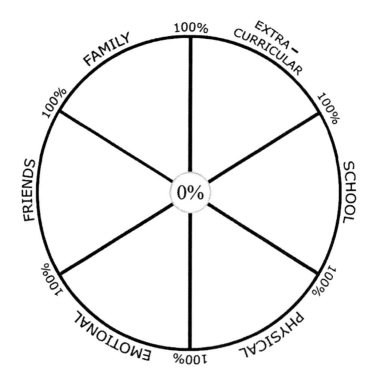

Think about it as a tire in your child's car called life. Based on the percentages in each section, how would the car run? What if it was going 20 mph? What if you had an achiever child who wanted to go 100 mph? How smooth could the wheel run if school was 100, extracurricular 40, and friends were 25? It's important to teach your children to balance their time, energy and focus into all areas that matter in life.

If you help your child put all these pieces of the puzzle together, you will raise a superstar who shines in every direction. I know you can do it. You will have easy days and challenging days. You will have times when you feel like a genius and other times when you wonder why you had kids in the first place. Keep at it. In the end, there is no more rewarding work in this life. Educate yourself, love your children and give them confidence, and you can't help but produce superstars!

Remember, I would love to hear from you. Send me your questions, thoughts or parenting wisdom to terri@RaisingASuperstar.com. You can also sign up for my free parenting tips and find out more about what I'm doing at www.RaisingASuperstar.com. Thank you for your time, your attention, and your trust. I wish only blessings for you and your superstars.

Printed in the United States
88138LV00003B/124-162/A